NORA

DATE DUE

Ireland Into Film

Series editors:
Keith Hopper (text) and Gráinne Humphreys (images)

Ireland Into Film is the first project in a number of planned collaborations between Cork University Press and the Irish Film Institute. The general aim of this publishing initiative is to increase the critical understanding of 'Irish' Film (i.e. films made in, or about, Ireland). This particular series brings together writers and scholars from the fields of Film and Literary Studies to examine notable adaptations of Irish literary texts.

Other titles available in this series:

The Dead (Kevin Barry)
December Bride (Lance Pettitt)
This Other Eden (Fidelma Farley)
The Informer (Patrick F. Sheeran)
The Quiet Man (Luke Gibbons)
The Field (Cheryl Temple Herr)
Dancing at Lughnasa (Joan FitzPatrick Dean)
Ulysses (Margot Norris)

Forthcoming titles:

The Butcher Boy (Colin MacCabe)

Ireland Into Film

NORA

Gerardine Meaney

CORK **CUP** UNIVERSITY PRESS

in association with
THE IRISH FILM INSTITUTE

First published in 2004 by
Cork University Press
Cork
Ireland

British Library Cataloguing in Publication Data
A CIP catalogue record for this book is available from the British Library.

ISBN 1 85918 291 7

Typesetting by Red Barn Publishing, Skeagh, Skibbereen

Printed by Betaprint Ltd, Dublin

Ireland Into Film receives financial assistance from
the Arts Council/An Chomhairle Ealaíon and the Irish Film Institute

For Ciara, Gráinne and Gerry

CONTENTS

List of Illustrations   viii

Acknowledgements   ix

1   Introduction   1

2   From Biography to Biopic   4

3   Filming the Living and the Dead   15

4   Trieste, Decadence and Location   29

5   Undressing the Costume Drama   31

6   Fetishism and Film Theory   38

7   An Other Desire: Screening Nora from Molly   59

Credits   77

Notes   80

Bibliography   85

LIST OF ILLUSTRATIONS

Plate 1.	Pat Murphy	5
Plate 2.	Brenda Maddox	6
Plate 3.	Nora in boy's clothing	11
Plate 4.	Nora at window looking down at Michael Furey	13
Plate 5.	Nora watching fight between Joyce and Stan	16
Plate 6.	Nora at the cinema, gazing at the screen	17
Plate 7.	Love scene (Joyce and Nora)	23
Plate 8.	Lucia looking through the banisters as Stan comes up	26
Plate 9.	Nora in a stunning hat	31
Plate 10.	Nora in her Dublin clothes	44
Plate 11.	Nora in her Triestine glamour	45
Plate 12.	Nora reading letter	46
Plate 13.	Nora poses for her portrait	50
Plate 14.	Prezioso reads Nora's images	52
Plate 15.	Joyce playing *The Lass of Aughrim*	72
Plate 16.	Nora reciting poem	72
Plate 17.	Joyce in bed listening to her recitation	73

Acknowledgements

I would like to thank Pat Murphy for her co-operation, helpfulness and generosity with her time and information in the preparation of this volume. In particular, I am very much indebted to her for an extended interview on 22 March 2003, much of the content of which is included below. Any statements of opinion remain, of course, my own, except where they are directly quoted from the interview material. This is a work of interpretation and so the relationship between it and the content of the interview is not always direct, but is, I hope, always engaged in dialogue. Any errors of fact are the responsibility of the author.

I was lucky enough to be able to teach the content of this volume on a variety of courses, which has contributed enormously to the development of the ideas therein. I am particularly grateful to several groups of lively, argumentative students at University College Dublin over the last few years, including those on the MA programmes in Film Studies, Anglo-Irish Literature and Women's Studies, for their comments, questions and especially disagreements. I am grateful to the following for the opportunity to discuss *Nora* in an international context: Anne Fogarty and the Joyce International Summer School; Tadhg O'Keefe and the University College Dublin International Summer School; Diane Negra and the Northern Illinois University/University of North Texas Media and Culture in Ireland Program. A special thanks to Valerie Hazette, Dervila Layden and Lorraine Stierle, who have been on related research journeys with me and have helped to keep the discussion of *Nora* connected to broader debates about the relationship between film and literature, contemporary Irish culture and gender in cinema.

Thanks are also due to the staff of the University College Dublin library and the Irish Film Archive for their assistance in the preparation of this book.

My thanks also to my former colleagues in the Centre for Film Studies at University College Dublin, especially Margaret Brindley, for technical and organisational support, wit and efficiency, and Ruth Barton and Harvey O'Brien for the opportunity to present a paper on *Nora* at the *Keeping It Real* Conference at University College Dublin. Special thanks to Lance Pettitt, Elizabeth Cullingford and Diane Negra for their most helpful responses to that paper. Thanks, too, to the Research Seminar of the Department of English for the opportunity to present a paper at the concluding stages of writing and to Danielle Clarke, Wanda Balzano and particularly Moynagh Sullivan for their comments and responses to that paper. My thanks also to Gráinne Humphreys for her very valuable assistance as visual editor. Special thanks to Sara Wilbourne for her warm encouragement to undertake and complete this project. I am also most grateful to staff at Cork University Press for their very practical assistance.

Thanks to my sister Norah for tolerating the oddity of my writing a book on her very near namesake.

As always, my thanks to Gerry Dowling, whose support and good humour keep me writing, and to Ciara and Gráinne for fun, distraction and a sense of perspective.

The editors would also like to thank Antoinette Prout, Ben Cloney, Stephen Moynihan, Sheila Pratschke, Lar Joye, Michael Davitt, Luke Dodd, Dennis Kennedy, Kevin Rockett, Ellen Hazelkorn, Seán Ryder, Paul Sinclair, St Cross College (Oxford), the Irish Film Institute and the Arts Council of Ireland. We owe a special debt of gratitude to Sara Wilbourne, the co-founder of the series, for her unflagging enthusiasm, integrity and commitment.

1

INTRODUCTION
....

Nora is in some respects closer to the biopic genre than to straightforward literary adaptation. However, the film credits its source as Brenda Maddox's biography, *Nora*,[1] and publicity for the film, and the re-issue of the book with a cover still bearing an image from Pat Murphy's film, re-enforced this relationship. Since the film's release, however, the differences in emphasis have become more and more apparent. The adaptation of the biography is merely a starting-point for the film, which engages in its own complex exploration of the relation between life and art in Joyce's early work. That exploration in turn raises issues about the way in which material existence is transfigured in art, the ethics of that transformation and the amorphous borders between manipulation and representation, specifically offering a feminist critique of high modernist aesthetics.

The film covers the initial period of the relationship between James Joyce and Nora Barnacle, ignoring the second half of Maddox's book. The film's preoccupation with the literary output of this period in Nora Barnacle and James Joyce's lives means that it offers not just a feminist revision of their biographies, but also a contemporary dialogue with Joyce's work. Hence the film needs to be set in a series of overlapping contexts: the Maddox biography of Nora, the demythologizing tendency current in contemporary Irish culture, Joyce's own writing, the import of historical melodrama as a genre within Irish film and the resurgence of the costume drama in the popular cinema of the 1990s.

The focus of this study is not on the film's fidelity to the attested biographical facts of either James Joyce or Nora Barnacle's life, but on the way in which it interprets them for a contemporary audience. Murphy's own view is that the film is not an adaptation in the usual sense, because it uses a variety of critical and biographical sources, particularly Joyce's letters and writings, as well as Brenda Maddox's biography.[2] Edna Longley has commented that Joyce made the journey from 'heretic to heritage' in one generation in Ireland.[3] Murphy's film pays due deference to the heretical bravery of its protagonists, but it is also an attempt to deconstruct 'heritage' Joyce. His anxiety that he might have been too hard on Dublin in his early work is too much quoted.[4] Against expectation, this feminist biopic of Nora Barnacle tries to rescue Joyce's reputation for a popular audience from the warm glow of nostalgia, which has submerged it in the tourist promotion of the city he fled. *Nora* is not governed by biographical exactitude. Instead it uses Maddox's biography of Nora as a starting-point for a reinterpretation and an interrogation of texts where Joyce most obviously incorporated versions of Nora's memories and stories into his work.

I want to situate the film in relation to broader debates about the work of women directors and the representation of women in film. The film's representation of sexuality is unusually well developed and challenging in the context of Irish cinema and its analysis of the psychodynamics of passion is unprecedented. While I am interested in this film's adventurousness, the sexual timorousness of most Irish cinema requires explanation. Part of the appeal of historical and costume drama is the investment of sexual relations with a degree of importance which is crucial to romantic narrative, but not always credible in a contemporary setting. Films such as *The Playboys* (dir. Gillies MacKinnon, 1992) and *A Love Divided* (dir. Sydney Macartney, 1999) indicate that Irish settings retain an aura of the romantic for international audiences because they offer the frisson of repression, albeit a repression which is overcome by passion and which occurs in an attractive rural setting. *Nora* disrupts the soft-focus, sanitized sexuality of these films with its representation of sexual intensity. It does not at all eschew romanticism, however, using elaborate costume, optimizing the visual romance of its Dublin and

Trieste settings and offering a concluding image of the couple walking off into the Adriatic sunset, with no apparent sense of irony.

In concentrating on Nora's relationship with James Joyce after they leave Dublin together, Murphy's 'epic of an intimate relationship' (as she herself describes it) shifts the ground of the representation of sexuality in Irish film. The sexual explicitness of the film works to this end in that it deploys the conventions of costume drama, creating a sumptuousness of scene, fabric and texture, all of which are integrated into the representation of sexuality itself without recourse to the deployment of repression as either frisson or narrative engine. Moreover, in adapting the story of Nora Barnacle and James Joyce's relationship the film engages with a dissident but powerful strand in Irish culture which specifically identifies aesthetic and sexual freedoms. This cultural current has been mythologized through the figure of Joyce and particularly his choice of exile. In important respects the film works within Joyce's emblematic status as the Irish artist at odds with Ireland. Interjecting itself into Joyce's use of Nora's voice and memories in his work, it attempts to open up a dialogue with a different and perhaps now more comprehensible Irish past.

Kevin Barry's study of *The Dead* in this series praised the tact with which John Huston, the film's director, steered the script away from the obvious Hollywood tactic of flashback to fill in the gap in the text where Gretta Conroy's memories of her lost love remain ineffable. *Nora* begins with a challenge to the fidelity which is, as Barry points out, the hallmark of Huston's adaptation. It puts Nora's imagined history into that gap. Murphy's film is an unfaithful rendering – a decidedly more Joycean strategy.

2

FROM BIOGRAPHY TO BIOPIC

Brenda Maddox's biography of Nora Barnacle, originally published in 1988 and much reprinted, was part of a movement in the late 1980s and early 1990s to recover the lives of actual and historical female figures from their obscurity relative to their famous male relatives and lovers. (The American subtitle was 'The Real Life of Molly Bloom'.) Thus part of the context for the renewed interest in Nora Barnacle is an international one, with biographies of, for example, Zelda Fitzgerald and Vivienne Eliot appearing during the same period. Brenda Maddox has since written accounts of the married lives of D. H. Lawrence and W. B. Yeats, which accentuate the importance of their relationships with their wives.[5] (As a sign of the times, she has most recently changed direction, producing a biography of another little-known woman, Rosalind Franklin, though Franklin is thankfully more significant for her research in molecular biology than her personal relationships.)[6]

This biographical tendency was linked to a broader interrogation of modernism and modernist aesthetics not exclusive to feminism. Given Joyce's predilection for the use of his own and Nora Barnacle's life as material for his art, the Maddox biography is highly informative about the sources of particular episodes in his work and even more so about the distance between the actuality and the fiction. Crucially for *Nora* the film, Nora the biography draws attention to the disparity between the circumstances of Nora's early life – and, especially, her early loves – and the way in which they have been mythologized within Joyce's work, particularly 'The Dead' and *Exiles*.

'Eveline' typifies the resistance of the stories in *Dubliners* to biographical interpretation. In the story, a nineteen-year-old Dublin girl plans to elope with a sailor called Frank. Eveline, too bound to the pieties of family and Ireland, too unsure of herself and her own desires, finally fails to step on to the boat, which is as emphatically associated with freedom and the future as Dublin is with claustrophobia and the past in the story. 'Eveline' draws heavily on Joyce's own experience waiting and wondering if Nora Barnacle would come away with him when he left Dublin for Trieste in 1904 (Plate 1).[7] In contrast to Eveline, as both Maddox and Murphy emphasize, Nora chose an uncertain future and her lover over any ties of kinship or convention. Eveline's preoccupation with her dead mother and the blight on her life brought about by her mother's last instruction to look after her ailing father are easily identified with the plight of Joyce's sisters, but they are also ghosts of his own past. The tragedy of the collapse of Eveline's desire for life and sense of attainable happiness lies in her representativeness. Hers appears a typical story, the literary tip of the iceberg of wasted lives, repression and despair which *Dubliners* so acutely renders.

Plate 1.   Pat Murphy

Nora Barnacle's ability to make her own choices and take a chance on her future differs radically from the protagonists of *Dubliners*, but differs also from twenty-first century preconceptions of the lives and characters of early twentieth-century Irish women. Yet Nora's story is in its own way just as representative as Eveline's. As Maddox points out, 'if Nora identified herself as a servant in any form, she would have been part of the largest emigrant category; female domestic servants from Connaught'.[8] Maddox observes that the major difference between James and Nora and the 37,413 other young emigrants leaving Ireland in 1904 was their choice of destination. In that context, Murphy's film can be seen as an exploration of a hidden women's history as surely as her earlier film, *Anne Devlin* (1984). It is partly a story of one among the many thousands of young, uneducated but often strong-willed women who voted with their feet against the constrained circumstances of their lives in Ireland and simply left. The volume of unaccompanied young women amongst Irish emigrants was quite exceptional: 'In the post-Famine period historians have noted that emigration from Ireland was markedly different from that in other countries. While families and young men emigrated from other European countries, an almost equal number

Plate 2.   Brenda Maddox

of men and women emigrated from Ireland. From the 1890s, women dominated in Irish emigration, except during war years.'[9] Luddy and McLoughlin argue that, in understanding the causes of this preponderance of women emigrants, 'economic motivation should not blind us to the personal expectations emigrants had for their new lives'. As in the case of Nora Barnacle, 'Irish women tended to emigrate to urban areas, which is hardly surprising given the negative sentiments they held about agricultural life'.[10]

In this regard, *Nora* is an unusual instance of the tendency in recent Irish films, and films set in Ireland, to recount hidden histories. It tells a story outside the paradigms of official history, but also outside those of contemporary Irish film's construction of the past. A large measure of this derives from the chief protagonist herself. Nora Barnacle still has a quality of unexpectedness about her. Much of what is most surprisingly contemporary about her character as represented in the film is painstakingly accurate. Commenting on this, Murphy argues that Nora is 'an entirely subversive figure. I think what the movie does is give a couple of angles on her, but it is just such a short period of her life. You can't say all that she was and all that she is.' Despite the differences in style from her earlier films, *Nora* is typical of Murphy's work in its commitment to challenging the most deep-rooted cultural and social preconceptions: 'I've had people say to me "I loved your movie, but of course it was such a fantasy because she wouldn't have the intelligence to say that." People just think she was a chambermaid that [Joyce] got caught up with and that he did the honourable thing by not dumping her.' This is a view to which the director takes considerable exception:

> It really staggers me – it's a class thing. People don't see that people can come out of any background and be phenomenal. Also there's Joyce's attitude to her – when you read the letters you can see that he is always writing to her as an equal. She is never just the literary man's wife or the wife

who is beneath him. He's always writing to her saying 'please read my book'.

Responding to an observation that her film is completely at odds with the dominant representation of what women in that era were like, Murphy comments: 'I think that I was just following her, she just did those things.' While acknowledging that 'events are totally subject to interpretation', Murphy insists that the film's depiction of Nora's strength of character derives from 'what did happen . . . She did run away, she did run away with him and she did stick with him. She did actually match what he did in terms of their relationship.'

This sense of Nora's integrity as a subject and of the radicalism of her relationship with Joyce is indicative of the director's objections to contemporary evaluations of their relationship as exploitative or hierarchical. Some audiences have been puzzled by Nora's decision to stay in what they see as an abusive relationship, and by Murphy's choice of this subject matter:

> One of the things that has been said to me, particularly in the United States, is why did you make a film about a woman who is being abused by this man and who stayed with him when she should have left. I keep trying to say this isn't what abuse is . . . sometimes that's one of the situations where representation lags far behind and isn't flexible enough to adequately mirror what women's lives were truly like.

Asserting Nora's difference from both contemporary and historical preconceptions of women and relationships, Murphy's work mirrors a current interest in the history of spaces of sexual dissidence and difference within Irish culture and society. 'I don't think she could have been that unique', Murphy comments. 'There must have been women – of course there were – who just refused to take the shit. Who were able to form decisions and create their own lives, the way women do all the time.'

While predicated on an awareness of a different history, exceeding the logic of social authority and submission, *Nora* also acknowledges the powerful repressive forces against which Nora and Joyce rebelled: 'Having said that, the weight of society on her makes the decisions much stronger,' says Murphy. That context makes it all the more surprising and impressive, given 'that they were together and they were not married', and the film repeatedly points out 'that she had to deal with the contempt of his friends'. Above all, the film claims for its heroine a high degree of sexual and personal initiative, which also gives her central narrative agency within the film:

> I think there is a little ambiguity about who it was that decided they should actually go away and live together. In the movie he's in this wavering state and she says 'take me with you when you go'. And when she says that she predicates the next movement in the narrative . . . It wasn't as if he feels compelled to leave Ireland and she just follows him.

Irish historical films have frequently set female characters at the heart of the narrative, endowing them with emblematic status as indicators of national identity and social change. Indeed, *Nora*'s prolonged development process coincided with the emergence of historical drama as the major narrative form within Irish cinema. During the 1990s, the combination of family melodrama and the 'heritage' setting represented a familiar if not always attractive Ireland, largely for the consumption of an international audience. Most of these films were set in the past: some simply look like the past. The difficulty that 'heritage'[11] films have in negotiating Hollywood conventions is perhaps inevitable, given their ambition to feel the frisson of past repression, separate it safely from present reality, and enjoy the scenery on the way. Moreover, the heritage which might expect to be celebrated seems inescapably fragile and dangerous, a contested space sometimes difficult to fix in time.

The more recent of these films perform a kind of cultural therapy for buried trauma, confronting the present with what it finds most troubling about the past within the secure setting of mainstream cinematic narrative. These conventions put the past at a distance, the distance between audience and screen becoming the distance between 'them', the oppressors of the past, and 'us', the horrified contemporary viewers separated – often by less than a generation – from social institutions and codes of conduct 'beyond belief'.[12] Current Irish preoccupation with the past often seems structured around a sense of bewilderment. Cultural commentators comment on how confusing the pace of contemporary social and cultural change is, but attitude surveys show a population happier in inverse proportion to the certainty of their beliefs.

The reception of both documentary and fictional renditions of the recent past indicates that nothing is more mysterious to the present than the sexual and religious practices of forty or fifty years ago. The very positive reception given to *Nora* by Irish commentators on its release emphasized both the high production values (highly significant in an information technology culture), but also a sense of relief at a protagonist whose sexuality was recognizable to a modern audience. Murphy's film provides a powerful sketch of the brutal suppression of Nora's sexuality and individuality in the opening minutes of the film. Here we see a teenage Nora, in love with a young man identified as Michael Furey, the name given to Gretta Conroy's lover in 'The Dead'. This is a significant departure from Maddox, who carefully excavates three young men who were composited into one by Joyce when he drew on his wife's account of her early life in writing 'The Dead'. Consequently, for viewers familiar with the story, the opening scene works as a specific commentary on both one of Joyce's best-known works and on the consummate Joycean adaptation to date, John Huston's version of 'The Dead'.

In order to get out to meet Michael Furey, Nora dresses as a boy, a habit of hers which Maddox attests to in her biography, though neither

Plate 3.   Nora in boy's clothing

she nor Murphy can fully account for this intriguing behaviour. The effect of it in the film is to identify her adolescent sexuality with androgyny, innocence and childhood (Plate 3). As Marjorie Garber points out in her study of cross-dressing, there is a tendency in Western culture for transvestite figures to appear suddenly on the margins of texts which appear to have nothing to do with cross-dressing or even gender difference.[13] Garber argues that the presence of cross-dressing in these texts indicates that other aspects of the subject matter in some way challenge binary and exclusive sexual or gender categories. *Nora* is of course concerned with gender difference, but the blurring of gender is surprising. Cross-dressing may be rare in Irish literature, but cross-voicing is not. The voicing of the nation as feminine is only the most laboured example of the articulation of the other sex by male writers, crucially in the modernist period. The validation of, for example, Molly Bloom's soliloquy or Brian Moore's *The Lonely Passion of Judith Hearne* (1955) or John McGahern's *Amongst Women* (1990) as the perfect articulation of Irish, or any other kind of womanhood, is a pre-emptive strike against the possibility of a different articulation by women themselves. It also suppresses acknowledgement of the permeability of gender boundaries, which facilitates such work. Voicing the other is indicative of a certain instability of the self: it draws attention to the gaps in the boundaries between the 'opposite' sexes. Perhaps this is the conflict or difficulty that destabilizes binary and fixed identities, which produces the fleeting glimpses of male legs beneath the literary petticoats of Irish modernism.

The inclusion of the biographical detail of her cross-dressing without explanation or comment has multiple effects on the film's representation of Nora Barnacle. Pat Murphy, expressing her delight in the fact of Nora's teenage transvestism and her own determination to include it, points out that: 'In the way the precredit sequence has been cut, Nora being dressed as a boy doesn't make narrative sense. You just see it. It says something about her recklessness, but it is not mentioned again.' This excess over narrative is commonplace in the representation of cross-dressing in cinema. While it may not have a plot function here, it certainly has an impact on characterization, establishing Nora as both wayward and subversive long before she met Joyce. In Murphy's words, it shows 'that she'll take risks, that she's amused by things, that she's not taking categories seriously'.

This easy and unstructured sexuality is brutally suppressed by Nora's uncle, who sends her mother out of the room and then beats the young Nora until she is terrified to continue her relationship with Michael Furey (Plate 4). These opening scenes in Galway are the closest things in the film to Maddox's book. Murphy acknowledges their somewhat telegraphic structure:

> The beginning sequence acts like a trailer for the rest of the film, in a way. It is very condensed from what was shot. You are introduced to Michael Furey; you see the two of them out at night and the uncle seeing her. Her uncle beats her and threatens her with the convent. The night before she's sent there you get the scene where Furey comes and stands

Plate 4.   Nora at window looking down at Michael Furey

under her window. The link comes more from Brenda
Maddox than from anything in Joyce.

There are differences, particularly in the age at which Nora is
depicted, but as Murphy points out, 'The changes are in the nature
of storytelling for film'.

The brevity of the sketch is facilitated by the centrality of its
context for so many other films, but it is also strategic. It
counterpoints the romanticization and nostalgia that is there in
Gretta Conroy's account of Michael Furey in 'The Dead' with very
brutal realities, but it also establishes that this is not an assertion of
'reality' over fiction. Murphy comments that:

> I truly don't think I was thinking there about setting up the
> relationship with Joyce's work. What I was thinking of in the
> initial fifteen- or twenty-minute sequence was setting up her
> character, showing she had a life before she met James Joyce,
> that she was formed as a personality before she met him.

While those familiar with Joyce's work will make an immediate
connection to 'The Dead', the central question for Murphy was:

How do you describe how she was before they met? How do you describe the person that he actually fell in love with? It establishes very early on that it is her movie, that she is the person we'll be following, even though there may be scenes where she's not present.

In developing the script, Murphy was conscious of trying to shift the narrative ground, not just of representations of the Irish past, but also of sexuality, particularly female sexuality:

I felt that, in terms of cinema, there had never been a really great love story that came out of Ireland. A lot of the movies I was seeing then had a narrative vision of erotic love as something forbidden and transgressional. No movie narrative seemed to be able to hold the notion that people could just be together, have this great passionate love affair and be together. There was always a level of punishment.

Within these prevailing representations of sexuality in Irish film, love was 'always thwarted or doomed'. Murphy's 'great desire in making the film was to make this love story that, while it did not have a conventional happy ending, showed the process that people went through'. Adapting the story of Nora Barnacle and James Joyce for the screen inevitably provoked questions about the cinematic representation of sexuality in general. What interested her most as a director, she says, was:

looking at the way cinema itself works with narrative in terms of dealing with desire. The way cinema deals with desire which it considers illicit or transgressive in some way is to punish the character. Something awful happens. It's like the narrative that is set up is not capable of being flexible enough to allow for different kinds of endings.

3

FILMING THE LIVING AND THE DEAD

Nora establishes at an early stage that this is not going to be simply the excavation of a 'real' woman's story from a dominant masculine narrative. The film also demands to be understood in the context of Joyce's own fiction. The concentration on the early years of their relationship means that the film is heavily focused on the circumstances surrounding the production of Joyce's early work, including *A Portrait of the Artist as a Young Man* and *Exiles*, but concentrating on *Dubliners*, with particularly explicit references to 'Eveline', 'Araby' and the concluding story, 'The Dead'. For, as Murphy repeatedly points out, making a film about Nora was always going to be inseparable from (re)reading Joyce. The film is 'playing with the fact that an audience is bringing all this information with them to the movie'. The challenge for the filmmaker was both to use that knowledge and to disturb and challenge the preconceptions implicit in it: 'on one level you're feeding that [knowledge], on another you are seeing what else can we do with it. Knowing that you, the audience, know that, what else can we, the film makers, do with it?'

At one of the key points of definition of the film narrative's relation to Joyce's work, Murphy gives cinema a fictionalized role in the motivation of her characters. For Murphy, the scene where Nora goes to the cinema in Trieste is crucial to the relationship between the film, the known biographical facts, Joyce's work and the role of Nora Barnacle in all three. The scene comes directly after a terrible scene when Nora is woken by Joyce being brought home drunk by Stannie, and she appears in the doorway just as Stannie, infuriated, physically attacks his brother (Plate 5). The film acknowledges how bad Nora's situation was at that point, then moves immediately to identify her as

Plate 5. Nora watching fight between Joyce and Stan

teller of her own tale. This narrative agency on Nora's part is identified with her fondness for the cinema. It is after a visit to the latter in this film version that Nora tells James Joyce of her first love in Galway. Murphy comments:

> What's interesting is how everybody feels they know what happened here. There's the John Huston film, *The Dead*, and then there's what's supposed to have actually happened: they're in Rome and things are going badly. They are missing their friends in Trieste and Joyce is working long hours in a bank. He brings her to see Shelley's grave and she is so moved by the story that she tells him about her young lover in Galway. And this is the basis of the story which he transposed into 'The Dead'.

It is into this over-determined context that the film proposes film itself as an agent of the narrative, as Nora's emotional response to the film to which she goes provokes her to tell the story of lost love (Plate 6). There are several consistent factors through the many versions of the story. In the factual biographies of Nora and Joyce, it is the story of the Romantic poet, Shelley, who provokes her story of her own youth.[14] In 'The Dead', it is a song, 'The Lass of Aughrim', a ballad of seduction and betrayal, that precipitates it (Huston's film follows this faithfully and very effectively). In *Nora*, it is again an experience of art that provokes Nora's nostalgic recollection, but the art of cinema has supplanted literature and music:

> I knew it wasn't going to work going to Rome and doing the Shelley stuff. This is a key moment, when Joyce realizes that she has had a love before him. He has believed himself to be her first love, that he has taken this unformed personality and given her his love and so he is the receiver of all of her emotions.

Nora's story precipitates the action in the second part of the film, defining Joyce's part in it:

> He realizes that something really deep happened for her and it wasn't about him. And that's an incredible thing for him to discover. It's a turning-point in terms of the movie

Plate 6. Nora at the cinema, gazing at the screen

because it's the beginnings of his paranoia in relation to her. It sets all that happens afterwards in motion.

As this is a biopic of Nora, cinema is, on more than one level, identified with her existence beyond Joyce's stories of her. 'What I wanted to do, I suppose', says Murphy, 'because I'm a filmmaker, was to use her love of cinema as something that provokes this memory, that she then goes from the cinema and tells him. So that's the way it works, that's why it is there.' As a director, Murphy was obviously challenged and interested by her awareness of the audience's curiosity about '*how* she is actually going to tell this part of the story?'

> I used to think, what is it like for an audience seeing this. I think if they know and they recognize the quotes, for them it's not a plot point or something new that's being revealed. They're not thinking about *why* is that in the movie, they're thinking about *how* it's working. I always think it is like going to see a ballet, something like *Swan Lake*, where you have the thirty-two pirouettes, and the audience are watching the prima ballerina and they're comparing her to other dancers, they're going twenty-eight, twenty-nine, is she going to make the thirty-two?

Murphy's explanation of the narrative strategy of the film is in terms of taking a new perspective, making the familiar different enough to question. She draws attention to the fact that the way she tells the story 'isn't true', but challenges her audience to 'look at it this way for the moment. It's an important scene for me. I think if it weren't there the whole movie just wouldn't exist in the same way.' Because of 'The Dead' and particularly because the film, *The Dead*, has become a kind of touchstone of Irish period drama *and* Joycean adaptation, this moment is also one which draws attention to the impossibility of telling a new story. It nonetheless insists that it is possible and important to tell the story differently.

Demythologizing Ireland

In contemporary biography, history, criticism, poetry and fiction by Irish women there is a very strong demythologizing tendency, challenging and reworking perceived notions of historical figures, reworking mythological ones, and re-writing literary stereotypes. It is almost a cultural dominant in contemporary Irish women's poetry, most notably in the work of Eavan Boland, Eiléan Ní Chuilleanáin and Paula Meehan and, more obliquely, Medbh McGuckian. Pat Murphy's earlier films, *Maeve* and *Anne Devlin*, are the strongest examples of this demythologizing tendency in Irish film and they share with the poetry the technique of juxtaposing myth and history in a way which undermines the authority of traditional images and celebrates a difference of view. The contrast between the avant-garde aesthetic of Murphy's earlier work and the adherence to the conventions of mainstream narrative cinema in *Nora* has been somewhat overstated. Murphy herself points out that *Nora* was 'always conceived of in a different way' to her three earlier films, *Maeve* (1982), *Anne Devlin* (1984) and *Rituals of Memory* (1977). The relationship between these works in her view is 'rooted in the development of a single voice making these movies'. Murphy, interestingly, modulates this apparent claim for *auteur* status in a way which situates each of the films within the broader cultural and political contexts of their making: 'Film directors are often seen as maverick *auteurs*, consciously pitting themselves against the mainstream world, but instead my experience is that directors are looking at the world all the time as the material with which we want to work'.

Murphy is highly conscious of the cultural, social and political contexts that condition her work: '*Maeve* could only have gotten made at the time it was made and *Anne Devlin* grew out of that'. The refusal of narrative and dialogic structure in *Maeve* was in any case in considerable contrast to *Anne Devlin*. Murphy has commented that in *Maeve* 'meaning is generated by juxtaposing scenes'. In *Anne Devlin*

19

the 'meaning comes within the duration of individual images'.[15] Murphy links this with the nature of the central characters in the films, contrasting Anne Devlin's capacity to hold things together with Maeve's constant challenging of situations. At the heart of *Maeve*, *Anne Devlin* and *Nora* is an interest on Murphy's part which, she claims, 'has become a cliché . . . looking at diaries and journals and women who are obscured by history'. She specifically links *Anne Devlin* and *Nora* in their oblique approaches to the canons of Irish history and literature. *Anne Devlin* she describes as 'enclosed. It doesn't show the rebellion, in the way that *Nora* doesn't show Joyce's writing directly.' Both 'deal with the intimacy of a domestic world', though Nora was a very undomesticated woman. Both films mark a shift from avant-garde to art house in Murphy's work. *Nora* remains close to the European art house tradition, in its attention to visual detail, the composition of scenes, its subject matter and its funding and distribution. The narrative structure is much more conventional than either of Murphy's previous films, however:

> I really felt Irish cinema needed . . . this love story. It is very complex and not doomed. It is epic in terms of the dark space it goes into, but it also has this domestic daily-ness in terms of raising children. It is a story where people don't die at the end, where they come though it. This had huge implications for the writing of the script.

Again, the specific issue of representation of sexuality is linked to broader ones about contemporary filmmaking:

> Feature film writing has become very rigidly codified. So many people are locked into the notion of the three-act structure. Finance people and script editors were coming back with 'your movie has two endings and you can't do that in a straightforward feature. Your movie ends when [Joyce] comes back, when they are reconciled after the first set of

letters'. But what is important is that Joyce revisits his
jealousy with heightened stakes with regard to Prezioso.

In this context, it becomes apparent that *Nora*'s script was a complex
negotiation between the challenge to the mainstream implicit in its
material, the need to raise funds and secure distribution and a
willingness to take on and try to subvert mainstream narrative
conventions. For Murphy, *Nora* 'was always going to be for me an
attempt to take that on, to subvert the kind of rules that have
become quite rigid in terms of scriptwriting, and in terms of that
kind of filmmaking'.

The shadow of three-act Hollywood structure none the less
inhabits certain elements of the narrative, and even the relationship
with certain of Joyce's texts, especially in focusing on the early part
of Nora's and Joyce's relationship and the construction of Nora's
return to Ireland in 1912 as a much more significant event than
Maddox proposes. While there may be thematic repetition, there is
also a clear exposition, development and conclusion to the romance
narrative. This may be an unconventional love story, but it is told in
the recognizable terms of a film romance. Narrative imperatives give
priority to Joyce's dramatization of his plight when he is without
Nora over any declared intention to leave on her part. According to
Maddox, Nora wanted Joyce to come with her in 1912, but he
decided not to for financial reasons. He, on the other hand, worked
himself into a fever of anxiety when he had not heard from her for
five days and concluded that she was abandoning him. Joyce then
persuaded his English-language pupil Ettore Schmidt (later to
become the novelist Italo Svevo) to pay him in advance for lessons so
that he could follow her. The film version collapses this into a later
and much more serious breach between them. As Murphy points out:

What is happening there is the collapsing of two historical
periods into one. In 1912 Nora goes back to Ireland, taking
Lucia with her, and Joyce follows with Giorgio because he

can't live without her . . . This is conjoined with Nora's later journey with the children when they were grown up, when she had basically had enough of Paris and Joyce's drunkenness and the endlessness of the book and all the rest of it. So she came back to Galway for this visit, it was after 1921 because the Civil War was on, and he sent her a letter saying: 'I will make arrangements for money to be sent to you if this is where you want to be.' Then she realizes that Ireland isn't an option and leaves again, this time for ever. For the purposes of making the film these two incidents were written to work as one.

This episode, which provides a narrative climax in the film, is an obvious case of the imperatives of narrative taking precedent over fidelity to detail. The change serves more than one narrative purpose, however. The closing scenes express a certain ambiguity about the relationship, mapping out quite starkly the limited options available even to a woman of Nora Barnacle's strength of character. As Murphy comments: 'That hinges on one image.' When Joyce tells Nora 'you can't live here', he is partly pleading with her, partly playing on her lack of options:

There's that scene in the bedroom where he says 'I just wanted to give you back your power over me', and she walks out and goes down to the street. And then it all plays in her face. She comes to a decision and you don't know what it is. The film then cuts back to him lying in bed and she gets into bed with him and they just hold each other. That's the end of it really. Then they leave for Trieste and he says, 'I haven't got the money for the journey.' Then there is the last long shot as they walk down the pier. It's just what filmmakers do. It is an attempt to take something that's very sprawling in terms of narrative, to take what you think is the meaning in all of that, and make it work.

This series of scenes works as narrative closure through an evocative repetition of images from the opening scenes in Galway, though Murphy insists this echo of the film's opening was not conscious on her part. Ending where it does, the film avoids the most negative aspects of the relationship. The drinking doesn't stop, it does drive him blind and it does affect their relationship. They do stay together, but this is certainly no romantic idyll. Yet the film's closing image is of the two lovers beginning again in the golden glow of the Trieste sunset (Cover illustration). Commenting on this, Murphy remarks on the persistence of the relationship:

> I don't think that's negative. Look, I think one of the great things about that relationship is that it endured, it was a lifetime relationship. It shifts around. Sometimes I think her options were so limited she couldn't have left him; sometimes I think this woman could have done anything. If it got to the point where she didn't want to put up with this anymore, she could have left. She would have found other

Plate 7. Joyce and Nora

ways to exist. I think people, particularly American audiences, are astonished because they wouldn't see any relationship going beyond that first hurdle, those first accusations. The fact that they lasted so long seems to them a radical thing in itself. One of the things that I like about the movie is the circularity. The last image is very romantic in one sense, but by this point you feel the weight of everything that's gone on in the past. I guess what I want to show is that there isn't the idealism and the innocence and naiveté they would have set off with the first time. The second time what holds them together is their experience. Sometimes this can be a negative thing, as when someone says 'this is our shared experience and you can't tell anybody else'. That is intimacy and secrecy as a kind of abuse. And he does that in a way, before the portrait scene and after the St Patrick's Day party he says 'we've done things together that don't make sense to other people'. Their privacy is one of the things that motors their erotic life together. I think that's one of the reasons why she doesn't leave – no, I think she doesn't leave because she loves him. But one of the things that happens is that people grow into the habit and experience of each other and I think they completely did this. It becomes part of the compost of their relationship, it enriches it, it's something they have done together and they've survived it, so they can go on having survived it. That's really what the ending is about.

Despite Murphy's sense of their heroic rebellion against the sexual and social mores of the time, even despite Joyce's role in artistic revolution, there is something profoundly depressing about their later lives. The almost spectral figure of little Lucia haunts the narrative, hinting at shadows looming, creating fissures in the film's romanticization of her parents (Plate 8). In this respect, the film follows Maddox's presentation of Nora's nurture of the dependent and clinging Joyce as implicitly depriving her children of her maternal resources. The use of historical sources put particular constraints on the exploration of female sexuality as well as offering rich symbolic and visual resources. The film's representation of Nora's occasional disregard for the welfare of her daughter is disturbing, complicating the film's romanticization of the couple's irresponsibility.

One of the themes running through Maddox's book on Nora is that, because Joyce was so needy, he prevented Nora from being a good mother. He simply used up too much of her energy. This interpretation by Maddox protects Nora from the blame for the couple's shortcomings as parents. When asked about this, Murphy agrees that built in to her narrative is the view that the intensity of the couple's relationship marginalized their children: 'The dynamic is always between Nora and Joyce and the children are peripheral to that.' The facts of Nora's life make a polarity between sexual expression and motherhood in the film inevitable:

> The scene people find shocking is that one where Nora masturbates and then Lucia appears in the doorway. The thing that struck me – and this does in a sense come from Maddox – is that here are these letters coming and going, Nora is distraught, here she is having dropped everything because of what Joyce is demanding and I'm thinking what is going on in this household, how is the child being fed, how is the child being minded, where is she getting the time to write the letters, where is she getting the time to think about all these things, and the sense is that her absorption is so strong that the child is sidelined. Also, what I was trying to do in the movie is give a sense of the future and the child's isolation in the future and the separation that Nora may have felt from her. That's implicit in it.

Here was a writer who could re-invent the English novel, but who

Plate 8. Lucia looking down through the banisters as Stan comes up

still could not avoid becoming his father, traumatizing his children – no matter how much he loved them – with his drinking, his inability to provide for them, his moving them from place to place, and putting himself always at the centre of all their lives. Nora, too, was strong enough to save herself from repression, violence and Ireland in general, to transform herself from chambermaid to the artist's muse, yet she appears to have been unable to impart her strength to empower and nurture her daughter. Murphy argues that the exigencies of art ultimately are to blame:

> The children of artists, they are never the primary focus. I can think of any number of children of artists that have had disastrous upbringings because their parents were focused on their painting or their writing or their film. I think Lucia is another example of that. Yes, I do think that's true.

It is to the film's credit that these shadows loom within it, even if they are not fully explored. *Nora* is not an exercise in hagiography, uncovering an admirable woman from her obscurity, though Murphy acknowledges that there was a time when audiences and critics expected just such an exercise:

There was a period when it happened in relation to feminist filmmaking, but also in relation to race and class. There is a period dominated by a need for some kind of hagiography, where the people who are oppressed have to be shown as embodying everything that's true and noble. A lot of people had difficulty with *Nora* because they said 'she's a bad mother, you showed her being a bad mother, why doesn't she leave him?' Their hearts are in the right place and they want this glowing kind of representation of motherhood . . . But you can't have such a failure of nerve as to pander to that. Jane Campion was criticized for *The Piano* because the main character doesn't speak and the whole project of feminism has been for women to have a voice. And I think that argument is a little stupid.

On one level Murphy dismisses this: 'It's just something that comes up, it's not anything you can take on board when you're making work'. On another level the film pre-empts it, offering a justification of its celebration of Nora and Joyce's flawed romantic epic in a discussion of 'Araby' between Joyce and the character of Prezioso. Prezioso is initially Joyce's friend and mentor, introducing him to Triestine artistic circles and encouraging his work. Later he falls in love with Nora, a circumstance which excites Joyce and which he seeks to manipulate for his own purposes. Prezioso is presented in a highly sympathetic light in the film and Nora leaves Joyce for Ireland in horror at the emotional havoc they have wrought on their well-intentioned friend. Prezioso is important in the film, not only in plot terms, but also as a measure of Joyce's ethical and artistic integrity. Having read stories from *Dubliners*, Prezioso is very impressed. Sitting in the sun outside a Triestine café with Joyce, he remarks that he feels he has been on holiday in Dublin. He then corrects himself, speculating that holiday is perhaps not the right word. Joyce suggests 'A nightmare, perhaps?' Prezioso argues that this is not so, for, despite Joyce's attempts to hide it, his love for the place is evident. Prezioso's favourite story is 'Araby', which he admires for its realization of a young boy's desire to give something extraordinary and exotic to the girl he loves. Genuinely puzzled, Prezioso asks, 'So tell me, why must the boy fail? . . . The hero weeps bitter tears and curses what he calls his vanity.' 'Reality', responds Joyce to this criticism, but Prezioso protests: 'In life it is not always so tragic. Sometimes love can discover a treasure as strange and as beautiful as this boy wants to find in 'Araby' and it's real. Nora. Wouldn't you say she is real?' At this, Joyce can only put up his hands and laugh. Being true to life then, it is suggested, involves recognition of the reality of strange and beautiful surprises.

4

TRIESTE, DECADENCE AND LOCATION

Joyce and Nora's cosmopolitan version of emigration is celebrated in
Nora, which engages with and celebrates the particularity of place in
a way only possible through location filming. The focus on Trieste
situates the film in that cultural space where there are only foreigners.
In this respect, of course, Nora Barnacle herself is paradigmatic.
Nothing is more Irish about Nora than her decision to leave Ireland.
The concentration on the city in Joyce's work, always problematic
and difficult for Irish nationalism to assimilate, is an intrinsic part of
that emigrant cosmopolitanism. Dublin, in Joyce's fiction, is
inalienably itself, local and particular, but also very like any other city
in important respects. Mapping *The Odyssey* onto Dublin, Joyce writes
'the nation's modernity as the event of the everyday and the advent
of the epochal',[16] writes Ireland as a modern, Western, nation with
all the paradoxes implied by that conjunction of terms. In placing
Joyce's work in the context of both his relationship with Nora and
exploring that relationship primarily in the context of its Triestine
development, Murphy's film honours that work's fidelity to particular
places, acutely realized, and to the experience of strangers.

Pat Murphy has emphasized her interest in the influence of Trieste
itself on the development of Joyce's work.[17] She cites the city's cultural
cosmopolitanism, Freud's sojourn there and, above all, its
multilingualism as providing a context for understanding the sources
of the late work, particularly *Finnegans Wake*. She recalls that, 'when
money apparently couldn't be raised for [the film] in its entirety, some
people suggested that it deal just with the Dublin part of their story'.
This would have made the film a much more recognizably Irish
production, but Murphy resisted, 'because what interests me was this

period in Trieste which was so key to his writing and so key to their lives'.[18] In mapping an Irish story on to a broader European context, *Nora* is both unusual and very much of its time. Murphy comments that it is 'a very Irish film but most of it was made in mainland Europe, Hamburg and Trieste'. This, she points out, was 'being led by Nora and Joyce':

> Once you make the decision to make the film, Nora and Joyce lead you. Because they went east to Europe not west to America, it follows that you are going to be dealing with the question of what it meant to be European at that time.

Interestingly, the film's funding similarly came from an eastward, European, direction rather than a westward, Hollywood, one, and in style and narrative it is closer to commercial European art house than to the Hollywood style of most recent Irish productions. As has been consistently the case for recent Irish productions, the story of how this film came to be made is as complex as any story told in the film itself. The funding sources of *Nora* set it in the context of art house and independent filmmaking, self-consciously European and asserting itself against big-budget Hollywood, but it observes all the conventions of mainstream narrative cinema. The role of Ewan McGregor as star/producer, as well as elements of the narrative and visual style, are all related to the production history and funding sources of the film. *Nora* indicates the current necessity for this sector to appeal, to some degree, to a more mainstream audience than heretofore. For this reason, it has been contrasted approvingly by many Irish reviewers with Murphy's earlier avant-garde work.

5

UNDRESSING THE COSTUME DRAMA

Nora relishes the particular pleasures of the costume drama, which are the excessive pleasures of the gaze, particularly in relation to clothes, and it subverts those pleasures, tearing off the clothes of the period quite literally to see the passions beneath. Murphy's films have always had an ambivalent relationship with history. One of the primary continuities of theme between *Maeve*, *Anne Devlin* and *Nora* is their deconstruction of the monolith of history, challenging what is known, particularly what is known about the Irish past. None of them offer a simple opposition to that knowledge in terms of the reality of experience, however. As Murphy points out, *Maeve* was criticized for showing 'feminism as this woman who has essentially a negative relationship to the characters and to her life, who is always

Plate 9. Nora in a stunning hat

questioning everything. She's not embodying a principle, she's questioning everything'. *Anne Devlin*'s narrative is reconstructed from her own diaries, yet it uses voice-over only once, in Anne's closing comments on the significance of her own silence and the refusal of those she had saved to recognize her. Respect for the integrity of the visual image dominates all of Murphy's work:

> I have a resistance to cinema that explains everything away. I like movies that have a kind of privacy about them so that you never get the full story about the characters. I think it's not good when everything is revealed to you. And with someone like Nora Barnacle you have to say I *think* this, this and this, but other things I don't really know about. So yes, it is true, you do want to leave her quite a lot to herself. (Murphy's emphasis)

The refusal to explain everything is, on the one hand, a legacy of the forging of her filmmaking practice in the avant-garde, anti-narrative 1970s. Yet in important ways it also signifies a refusal of the formalist mode dominant at that time. In the introduction to her 1996 re-formulation of feminist film theory, Laura Mulvey comments:

> History is, undoubtedly, constructed out of representations. But these representations are themselves symptoms. They provide clues, not to ultimate or fixed meanings, but to sites of social difficulty that need to be deciphered, politically and psychoanalytically . . . even though it may be too hard, ultimately, to make complete sense of the code.[19]

Murphy's filmmaking retains a commitment to sites of social and cultural difficulty, but also to code breaking. As such it offers a highly productive context for an examination of the divergent trajectories of feminist film theory and feminist filmmaking in the closing decades of the twentieth century. Re-inventing the costume drama, filmmakers like Jane Campion and Pat Murphy[20] have laid siege to a film genre where that most deplored engine of bourgeois ideology, fetishism, reaches its apotheosis. What they do to the genre has far-reaching consequences for the way in which women in film and as filmmakers are discussed.

The early influence of feminist film criticism, in particular, and film theory's general suspicion of visual pleasure has always been countered by the sheer visual aplomb of Murphy's work. Her films are almost painterly in their effect and this visual aesthetic is allied with a sumptuousness of design. The glorious light of Trieste and the contrasting grey half-lights of Dublin give *Nora* its distinctive feel of romanticism both stripped bare and reconstructed. As in Campion's *The Piano* (1993), Murphy uses a genre, the costume drama, which is often derogatively referred to as the 'women's picture'. This genre traditionally contained historical narratives in personal stories, privileging personal and subjective motivations and experience over social and historical context as a way of interpreting human experience. The use of the costume drama by the current generation of women filmmakers, however, can sometimes very successfully effect a feminist reversal, politicizing the personal and illuminating the way in which individual actions and desires, love affairs and families are shaped by social forces beyond individual control. There is a paradox here though, for such films focus on women who in some way defy or challenge the forces of convention, like Nora Barnacle or Ada in Campion's film.

Throughout *Nora*, Murphy avoids a simple opposition of historical fact to literary representation. This sense that Nora and her story cannot be fully known is related to the film's treatment of the past in general. The adaptations, transpositions and downright changes of the story from the attested facts for narrative affect have an effect beyond narrative cohesion. The way in which *Nora* is structured seeks to release a historical narrative from the burden of determinism. One of the problems of historical narrative is the sense of inevitability, which is a consequence of the knowledge that all of this has already happened and is known to have happened. Yet Nora and Joyce's story, as Murphy sees it, does not have this sense of closure: 'It's not just a love affair that's long over, we're actually interested in how modern Joyce is, just how incredibly modern that writing is and how modern their situation is. Yet visually it's rooted so much in a particular period.' The history of the process by which *Nora*'s final narrative form was determined indicates the priority which Murphy gave to offsetting the sense of inevitability and maintaining the sense of surprise and unexpectedness in the story. In an answer to a comment by this interviewer that many Irish films would have ended with them simply getting on the boat – or dying horribly on the way there – Murphy expanded on her choice of a different form of narrative: 'That could have been an ending. But the question of the ending was always huge as the film was being made.' Initially she had 'wanted to end the film with the publication of *Ulysses*, because I wanted it to end on the evening of his great triumph when Sylvia Beach has rushed to collect two copies from the railway station so Joyce will have it on his fortieth birthday in 1922. That always seemed to me to be such an extraordinary moment.'

Such a broad historical scope would have had major narrative implications, however, as Murphy wryly acknowledges: 'It would have been a six-hour movie.' This would have necessitated a very different narrative structure, comprising a series of episodes from their lives, possibly presented in flashbacks:

> Another way that I explored doing it would be to show a much older Nora in the guesthouse in Zurich. It would start after his death when she was back in the place where they started out and we would see the events in flashback. Not only were there several possible endings, there are a number of possible starts when you look at the story. There's where they meet in the street. There's where she supposedly makes him a man; he always thinks back to that moment. There's

> when they go to Zurich, and when they arrive in Trieste. So
> it seemed to me that one of the ways to structure the film
> could possibly have been around where she ends up, because
> that was also the beginning.

This sense of circularity in their relationship does persist in the final version of the film, ending with them starting out again on their initial journey. The reason for abandoning the retrospective, flashback narrative framework 'had to do with the sense of the audience as much as anything else. I think when movies tell stories in flashback it is structured as something contained and something that is definitively in the past, whereas I wanted the audience to experience what the characters were going through in the moment.' The first concept of the script, organized around memory and reflection, was accordingly drastically revised by Murphy, as it risked becoming 'too much of a bourgeois elegy – lost time, memory and this lost love'.

Murphy's account of the script's development bears comparison with the approach to history, relationships and the history of relationships in the adaptation of *December Bride* (dir. Thaddeus O'Sullivan, 1990). In his account of that process, Lance Pettitt comments that, in the original novel, 'the structure . . . is effectively that of an extended flashback, so we know from the beginning how the narrative will provide its own closure'.[21] Pettitt demonstrates how the adaptation attempts to open up this closed structure, providing 'an important fictional means of remembering that community's history differently, seeing how some within it dared to defy convention, question custom and imagine an alternative if not a perfect future for themselves'.[22] *Nora*'s protagonists were more daringly defiant. The film can certainly be identified with the project of radical historical filmmaking outlined by Pettitt, a project which Murphy's *Anne Devlin* pioneered in the Irish context. It also exceeds this agenda, however, imagining an alternative past in which a future based on a dis-remembering of tradition and custom could be based.

There are problematic elements in this attempt to avoid determinism and indeed to celebrate the assertion of freedom and sexuality. One is the extent to which the social and historical constraints on the exercise of both becomes obscured. 'I remember the actors asking me why won't she sleep with him', says Murphy, 'why do they wait till Zurich? Why is she so open with him in some ways and in other ways not at all?' It reminded her that:

> Modern people, born from the seventies on, don't have a sense of her fear of getting pregnant, which must have been huge for women in terms of having a sexuality in those days. People think it is some sort of personal decision about why you would be open and why you would close. It must have been huge for her.[23]

Asked if the decision not to represent Nora's fear of pregnancy is part of the film's attempt to break the mould of the way Irish historical films deal with sexuality, Murphy is adamant that it is not:

> No, it has not got to do with that, it is to do with not explaining everything about her, not being entirely aware of what her emotions and motives are, seeing the surface only. Sometimes in terms of film it is stronger if you don't actually have what is available to a novelist, someone can be a much stronger character if you don't exactly know what he or she is doing or why they are doing it. It is more mysterious and enigmatic. And I wanted to leave her with that. You don't always have access to what she thinks.

The difficulties of not explaining and the commitment to allowing elements of the past to remain unknown is indicative of a complex approach to period drama, which needs to be put in the context of broad debates about film, gender and history. *Nora* does not merely excavate an individual and particular woman from literary and historical representation. The question of female desire and women's 'place' in the cultural aesthetic of modernism is also being asked.

6

FETISHISM AND FILM THEORY

Discussions of the costume drama genre have focused primarily on the fetishistic function of clothes within costume drama and the related role of fetishism in film. Fetishism has been a highly influential concept in developing theories of how film works as a system of representation. There are two major definitions of fetishism: one psychoanalytical, the other with its origins in Marxist theory. Freud identified fetishism as symptomatic of arrested sexual development, specifically in males. The function of the fetish object for Freud was the denial on the part of the masculine fetishist of the 'fact' of the absence of male sexual organs from the mother's body; that is to say, in Freud's terms, a refusal to acknowledge that the mother is castrated. As Freud proposed it, the realization of the mother's castration both de-mystified her power and galvanised the son to identify with the father, and the only model for mature male sexuality that Freud's society recognized as appropriate: i.e. a very straightforward heterosexuality. Thus masculine heterosexuality was based on the identification of female sexuality with absence, lack and castration. In this view of sexual development, the absence of visible external sexual organs in women was more or less equated with the absence of female sexuality. Male heterosexual desire was also predicated on fear, or, more precisely, on castration anxiety, the fear of the mother's fate overcoming the son. While this model of sexual development may seem outrageous to a contemporary readership, particularly read from the perspective of women's sexuality, it is important to acknowledge the roots of Freud's theory in deep structures of power and sexual inequality within the traditional Western nuclear family. It is this insight into fundamental fears, anxieties and structures of sexual difference which has proved so influential on theoretical work seeking to analyse and change culture, media and society. Laura Mulvey's ground-breaking essay on 'Visual Pleasure and Narrative Cinema' in 1975, for example, argued that Freud's theory accounted for the cinematic construction of woman as the object of the gaze, displayed to be looked at but signifying only absence, castration and lack. In film, the film image is both desired and feared.

Freud's theory of fetishism identified a range of objects which substituted for the disturbing female genitalia and offered gratifications he was quick to diagnose as perverse, as they did not lead to reproductive sex. Freud also acknowledged, however, that culture itself may emanate from this particular perversity. After all, cultural forms depend on the fetishistic principle of substitution and displacement, through representation. The relationship between fetishism and representation was explored along these lines in Jacques Lacan's re-reading of Freud. Lacan integrated the insights of twentieth-century linguistics into psychoanalysis. Fetishism ceased to be a curable perversity and became an indicator of the basic functioning of systems of representation, primarily language. Language – and consequently subjectivity, communication and society – is only possible because we learn to substitute the sign for the thing itself.

There are parallels in Marxist theories of fetishism. In these accounts, fetishism is once again a strategy of denial, though this time that which is denied and rendered invisible in the process of fetishization is the labour which produces the commodity. The commodity then becomes a fetish, a substitute imbued with value beyond its use and with symbolic power. Commodity fetishism obscures the social nature of the value of a commodity. It obscures the extent to which value derives from what we are prepared to pay and substitutes the illusion that the value is intrinsic to the commodity. Commodity fetishism is particularly evident in our desire for objects which have no apparent use or where the object's value is disproportionate to its usefulness or the cost of its production. High art has long been the ultimate commodity fetish, where the adjective 'priceless', in fact, denotes a very high price determined by the desirability of a rare object in a competitive market. Designer goods are a highly fetishized example in our culture, to the extent that the conditions of their production (e.g. by low-paid workers in the developing world) and their practical use (e.g. as no more nor less than an item of footwear, clothing or tableware) are entirely obscured by their social meaning (e.g. good taste, high standards, lifestyle choices, prosperity, belonging). In such highly prized goods, Marx originally argued, relations between things are substituted for relations between people.

Sexual fetishism often bridges the gap between the psycho-analytical and Marxist models. The fetish objects as described by Freud are often (though not always) also expensive commodities, such as fur, velvet and ornate shoes. The current craze for Manolo Blahnik's designer shoes is a glorious example of the difficulty of disentangling the gratifications of unbridled consumption and sexual fetishism, not least because they are desired by women on the basis that they signify desirability. The elaborate clothes fetishism in Joyce's letters to Nora and in Murphy's use of the conventions of costume drama need to be understood in both contexts.

While serious studies of the costume drama have been relatively rare,[24] the psychoanalytical concept of fetishism and, latterly, analyses in the Marxist mode of commodity fetishism have been central to the understanding of the genre, as they have been to the development of feminist film theory. What I want to do here is to explore the relationship between costume drama, fetishism and feminist filmmaking. Stella Bruzzi's analysis of the role of costume design in *Undressing Cinema* is particularly relevant to understanding *Nora* in the context of the treatment of gender and of history in contemporary cinema. Bruzzi reviews the resurgence of the costume drama at the end of the twentieth century. She sees Peter Weir's *Picnic at Hanging*

Rock (1975) as an important watershed for the genre, but she identifies the film with a highly conventional fetishistic construction of costume and of femininity itself. Her reading of this particular film is very close to the general construction of the cinematic gaze in Mulvey's enormously influential article from the same year as Weir's film, 'Visual Pleasure and Narrative Cinema'. There, Mulvey had placed fetishism and scopophilia (sexual gratification through looking) at the centre of both psychoanalytic and feminist film theory to the extent that any other forms of film theory have had to define themselves against that formulation since. Mulvey has in recent years been unreserved in situating her theoretical breakthroughs within their own historical and cultural context, pointing out that:

> In the early seventies my argument was, by and large, formalist, and only in retrospect, perhaps, is its very restricted historical focus clear. It was about the cinematic specificity of the Hollywood, post-synchronised sound, studio system, and way of depicting sexual difference. It was not, therefore, about complex modes of identification or subject positions. It was not about the possibility of an individual's sophisticated negotiations with a chosen sexual fantasy as elaborated within psychoanalytic theory. It was not about the gaze in psychoanalytic theory as such, or about seeing in any aesthetic or social context other than that suggested by certain Hollywood genres. 'Visual Pleasure and Narrative Cinema's' formalism has, of course, often been criticised, particularly by those who argue that an audience asserts its own social identity over and above the formal construction of the spectator. But those were the utopian days of the early seventies, when a formal, but political critique of Hollywood went hand in hand with a formal, but political concept of a new radical cinema. And the Women's Liberation Movement directly influenced both.

Its context was, in other words, precisely the one that also made *Maeve* possible. It was also a moment when the boundaries between radical filmmaking and radical analysis of film were much less clearly defined than today. Mulvey's later amalgamation of Marxist theories of commodity fetishism into the psychoanalytical construct in her 1996 *Fetishism and Curiosity* offers a far more political historicization of fetishism than that with which she is generally credited. Responses to the book on the *Film–Philosophy* website foregrounded both this strength of the book and its correlative weakness, the underdevelopment of a sense of an (historical) audience. Murphy's concept of the role of the filmmaker may even offer a route out of the theoretical impasse of text-based versus audience-based interpretation, given her understanding of the 'notion of integrated practice'. She argues that filmmakers are 'uniquely . . . thinking of the audience all the time, thinking about the audience as almost an element within the movie. The rhythms of the film only make sense when an audience is responding to them.' Thus in *Nora* a dual interaction takes place between the film and its Joycean sources, and the film audience's preconceptions from and of those sources.

Fetishism and Costume Drama in the 1990s

Bruzzi's deployment of the concept of fetishism in cinema shows the direction in which feminist film theory has developed since the utopian seventies, often in response to developments in the work of women filmmakers. Weir's film is identified by Bruzzi as:

> an exclusively male fantasy in which representation, symbolism and narrative converge to evoke the (adolescent) male obsession with the female sexual object. The female is both central and absent . . . The only viable position for the female spectator is as an enigma-identifier; to desire to be the absented object with whom everyone is infatuated, to desire to be the fetish.[25]

In Bruzzi's reading, *Picnic at Hanging Rock* is symptomatic of the masculine fetishism at the heart of the cinematic apparatus. She argues that *The Age of Innocence* (dir. Martin Scorsese, 1993) indicates that the 1990s costume drama moved beyond this enactment of fetishism. Distance from an unobtainable feminine object is still the organizing principle of narrative and cinematography, but, in the allusive tradition of film melodrama, 'the intensity of the desire is deflected onto the film image itself'.[26] In *The Age of Innocence* the past itself is the distant, fetishized object, but it is a very particular past. Bruzzi argues that the film 'is the clearest example to date of Scorsese's fetishization of cinema history'.[27] It is a post-classical elegy for the intensity and newness of the cinematic image presumed lost. Both the sense of cinematic presence and its loss are evoked in stylistic references to Ophuls, Eisenstein and Sirk. While it shares many of the melodramatic features of Sirk and Ophuls, *The Age of Innocence* does so at a distance and within the framework of an acknowledgement of the past as beyond recovery and identification:

> The past is made strange in *The Age of Innocence* through an obsessive attention to minutiae and authenticity, as if the spectator had been invited to observe the meticulous dissection of late nineteenth-century manners, cuisine and clothes in order to both revel in them and recognise their role as signifiers of that society's extreme superficiality. The fetishized object thus simultaneously represses and renders visible the implied desire.[28]

This is a sublime fetishism: its pleasures are dependent upon the self-conscious recognition of the impossibility of realizing its desire. It is distant not only from its object, but from itself.

Asked about her film's relation to costume drama, Pat Murphy acknowledges it is unusual within that genre in that it uses the past as a context for sexual expression rather than repression. Consequently, the fetishization of the past through the meticulous period authenticity which characterizes most 'period' drama is disrupted in *Nora*. The film celebrates Nora and Joyce's use of clothes as a form of sexual expression; like *The Piano*, it 'adopts clothes and their relationship to sexuality and the body as primary signifiers'.[29] Bruzzi identifies this in *The Piano* with its 're-examination of and . . . counter-argument to the conventional views of nineteenth-century sexuality'.[30] In *Nora* it offers a direct challenge to the construction of the history of Irish sexuality.

Murphy is very clear about the unwillingness of the past to stay past and safely contained in *Nora*. She says that for her there are two ways of looking at the significance of costume in the film. 'One of them is very simple. She starts out as a girl as this neat chambermaid' (Plate 10). Then she becomes a very different woman (Plate 11): 'In a scene which I think is one of her best in the film, Stannie is looking around her new apartment as she reads a letter from Joyce in the background' (Plate 12). As the scene develops, a dissonance emerges between what is seen and what is said:

Plate 10. Nora in her Dublin clothes

Plate 11. Nora in her Triestine glamour

> There's the gap between how elegant [Nora] looks and how
> wounded she is by this letter and then how hard and crude
> she is when she says, 'Go on, read out where he asks who else
> fucked me before he did.' The film is very situated then and
> an incredible amount of work goes into getting the detail
> right, and then suddenly the language that they use seems
> so modern.

One of the effects of these moments when the past and present
interrupt each other is that, however beautifully costumed, Nora
never becomes what Mulvey describes as a 'carapace' of femininity in
the film. Mulvey's work has persistently drawn attention to the
contrast between the screen idol, the image of the female star, and the
violent repudiation of female power in classic Hollywood cinema; to
those moments 'when the exterior carapace of feminine beauty
collapses to reveal the uncanny, abject maternal body'.[31] At these
moments 'it is as though the fetish itself has failed'. That dichotomy
between the feminine exterior and abject interior is avoided in this

Plate 12. Nora reading letter

film through the medium of Nora's voice, which ruptures the carapace from within.

In this context the film's casting is significant. Murphy from the start wanted a recognizable male actor and a relatively unknown female one. This works on several fronts. Ewan McGregor's star quality makes sense of the narrative for a contemporary viewer unfamiliar with the context. He presents a plausibly charismatic figure capable of manipulating others in the service of his higher artistic purpose. Like all stars, McGregor also brings a specific set of meanings derived from his previous roles to the part. In his case these include unpredictability, an ability to move between Hollywood and independent projects and a contemporary, ambivalent version of male sexuality. In a manoeuvre very flattering to Joyce's memory, the artist is cast in the role of the object of another's desire (Plate 17). The casting of Susan Lynch as Nora Barnacle accentuates this. Lynch has a riveting screen presence, but she is far less well known than McGregor. Consequently, she, rather than McGregor, fits the role of filtering consciousness, the point of identification for interpretation of the narrative, much more easily. Her performance exudes a confident female sexuality, but McGregor's star persona signifies an unconventional male one. Murphy has remarked that it was McGregor's performance in *The Pillow Book* (dir. Peter Greenaway, 1996) which convinced her of his suitability for the role of Joyce. It can hardly be coincidence that McGregor's character in that film is an object of erotic exchange on whom the text of an (female) other is inscribed. In producing 'an unconventional representation of masculinity as the object of the female gaze', *Nora* invites comparison with the final film in the triad of costume dramas discussed by Bruzzi, Jane Campion's 1993 film, *The Piano*:

> *The Piano*, in offering a representation of the past from a clearly feminine perspective, posits the notion that fetishism is not exclusively applicable to men. Campion's film suggests that superficially restrictive clothes function as equivocal signifiers, acting both as barriers to sexual expression and as the very means of sexual fulfilment.[32]

Bruzzi argues that the feminine fetishism in operation in *The Piano* is, in opposition to the many definitions of masculine fetishism, characterized by the attempt to bring the object of desire closer, rather than maintain controlling distance. This is a fetishism of love rather than dominance.

Looking Differently

While our general understanding is that the (human) subject is active, looking at, interpreting and identifying the object of its gaze, Lacan's revision of Freudian theory offers a different perspective. As Lacan describes it, attainment to the position of the subject is precipitated by the recognition of one's 'self' in the mirror stage. There is a literal dimension to this: the infant learns to recognize an image in the mirror as him or her self. Consequent upon this, the infant identifies him/her self as an autonomous, separate entity. This is a self-flattering fiction, for the image in the mirror is in fact far more coherent and integrated than infants, whose motor skills are still developing, experience themselves to be. The self from the start is more of an aspiration than a reality. Gradually the subject assumes this autonomous self to be not only coherent and unified, but also in charge of his or her own choices. Lacan's description of the mirror stage is also a metaphor for development in the context of the child's relations to others. Perhaps more significant than the physical mirror is the role of others' perception in mirroring back to us an image which we accept as our own. The crucial other in the traditional child-rearing practice of the Western family is the mother. The closeness of mother and child and the infant's dependence on her make the process of separation highly fraught. The mother is the other in which the child perceives the strongest and most positive image of him or her self reflected back, but she is also that from which the child must separate in order to become that separate 'self'. The ability to use language, the ability to say 'I', is dependent on both recognizing the self in her image and losing through separation the (m)other. The pleasures of substitution and re-connection offered by language are then fetishistic pleasures, rooted in the denial of that loss and separation. In Lacan's original formulation, this ensures that the position of subjectivity in language is intrinsically masculine, regardless of the sex of the subject. This relationship between gender and language is crucial to Joyce's endeavours to produce a language which is not separated but which is specifically embodied and feminine.

Language and the Body: From Molly Bloom to ALP
It has become commonplace to regard Molly Bloom's monologue as not only the essence of feminine writing,[33] but also as the novel's final attempt to produce in writing a form of, or fusion with, the oral. Declan Kiberd makes a more radical assertion:

> *Ulysses,* judged in retrospect, is a prolonged farewell to written literature and a rejection of its attempts to colonize

speech and thought. Its mockery of the hyper-literary Stephen, of the writerly talk of librarians, of the excremental nature of printed magazines, is a preparation for its restoration of the human voice of Molly Bloom; and, in a book where each chapter is named for a bodily organ, the restoration of her voice becomes a synecdoche for the recovery into art of the whole human body.[34]

A site of recovery from literature, a textual embodiment of the negation of literature, Molly becomes, in this reading, the pre-Oedipal regained by the son *in his own words.* The anxieties and loss implicit in national and sexual differences are recovered in *Ulysses'* language which suspends the fall from senses to sense. Such euphoric identifications indicate success in consummating the perilous modernist romance with the phallic mother. Lack is lost in the embodied word. For Molly's soliloquy is, after all, not oral but a masterpiece of oralization, an appropriation of the oral rather than a surrender to it by the written word: 'a reunion with the mother's body which is no longer viewed as an engendered, hollow and vaginated, expelling and rejecting body, but rather as a vocalic one – throat, voice and breasts; music rhythm, prosody'.[35]

Like the cultural nationalists he challenged, Joyce finally makes a version of the feminine a guarantor of his new (literary) order. Yet, at the end of *Ulysses,* the exile finds home a strange enough place. Dublin is itself a fetish of Joyce's writing, the object which has to be lost in order to be reconstituted elsewhere in language, desired and resented. As such, the representation of Dublin and the relationship between home and abroad, alienation and cosmopolitanism, is inextricably linked with the relations between the sexes in Joyce's work.

Precisely because Joyce's later work provides one of the most compelling investigations in twentieth-century literature of what it is to be in language, its role in the constitution of human subjectivity and the relation of both to sex and gender, any film which hopes to engage with Joyce's work is compelled to engage with fundamental questions about the nature of representation, what is represented, and by and for whom. Within film this necessitates an investigation of the relationship between looking and being looked at.

Within Lacan's theory of the subject, what Murphy, Campion and other feminist filmmakers do is impossible. This impossibility of the female gaze was the keystone of the first phase of feminist film theory. In important respects it is also the predicate of feminist filmmaking. The only radical response to the construction of the gaze and of subjectivity in exclusively masculine terms is to rupture the boundaries of possibility and look as a woman anyway. The portrait scene at the heart of *Nora* dramatically exposes this logic. Initially, Nora is posed, presented as the object of the gaze of painter, husband and potential lover. She is their common purpose and the fixed still focus of their attention (Plate 13). Each of them sees a different Nora. There are strong parallels with the crucial point in

Plate 13. Nora poses for her portrait

'The Dead' where Gabriel Conroy looks up the staircase to see his wife, Gretta, standing above him. He looks at her as 'his wife', secure in his relationship to her and valuing her almost as an object of art: 'He asked himself what is a woman standing on the stairs in the shadow, listening to distant music, a symbol of. If he were a painter he would paint her in that attitude.'[36] Gabriel is completely unaware that she is remembering another, long-lost love. He assumes that she is a symbol of something outside herself, a meaningful object. The rest of the story reveals she is searching for the meaning of her own past, her memories provoked by her own active aesthetic engagement with that distant music.

Setting Nora up as both an object of art and as the object of another's affections, Joyce in this film becomes Gabriel Conroy precisely because he is trying so hard not to be. He tells Nora he wants to give her back her power over him, but in fact he is looking for a higher artistic power than that which finds symbols at the top of the stairs, one based on the embrace of uncertainty rather than security. He still assumes the power to assign their roles to others and to assign meaning to them through his art. Consequently, in this scene, Nora is set up initially as a discursive object. The relationships between Joyce, Prezioso and the painter are all negotiated through their relationships with her. At least in this scene, they define her, it seems (Plate 14). But Nora is neither their other, the opposite against which they can define themselves, nor their object, defined by their gaze upon her. She plays and then refuses her role as a projection of their fantasies and, in a gesture which draws attention to the difference between painting and filming, Nora rushes out of the frame. The dynamics of the scene go beyond an attempt to reformulate the binary relationships of active subject and passive object. For the scene is constructed to imply a critical feminine/feminist subject who occupies the position of unattributed point of view, the authoritative position of all-knowing subject in the language of film. From this perspective, we are shown a group of

Plate 14. Prezioso reads Nora's images

male artists and critics looking at a woman who ultimately refuses their gaze.

The importance of historical change is the crux for the significance of fetishism within film theory. Bruzzi's reading of *The Piano* introduces the possibility of historical change in the role of fetishism. That possibility has been occluded in most psychoanalytic theories of fetishism (particularly fetishism in film) on two levels. Firstly, in Freud's originary texts on this topic, the fetish is a symptom of arrested development. The gaze of the desiring subject is frozen in its misperception of castration, its disavowal of sexual difference and refusal of 'normal' sexual development. Fetishism is both a relation of dominance over the fetishized object and one of subjection to the mystery of the phallic mother, but it is nonetheless, in Freudian terms, infantile. The construction of fetishism thereafter in Lacanian theory is as a universalized structure, where a myriad of specific and distinct fetish objects are subsumed into a single fetishistic function. This assumption of the irrelevance of the actual fetish objects assumes that the same function is fulfilled and the same effect realized by, for example, the velvet and furs that pervade Freud's case histories and Joyce's letters on the one hand and the piano and torn stockings in *The Piano* on the other. Fetishism becomes an empty signifier which 'can be filled in by a new particular content'.[37]

Yet nothing is more historically determined than the fetish. Reading Joyce's pornographic letters to Nora for the first time provoked in me an immediate suspicion that he was parodying Freud. Somewhat disorientated, I checked the dates of *The Three Essays on Human Sexuality* (1905) – 'On the Genesis of Fetishism' (1909), and 'Fetishism' (1927) – just to reassure myself it could not be so. Even though Freud's first observations on fetishism precede the first group of letters by four years, there is no evidence that Joyce was familiar with them when he began his correspondence. Yet these very private letters reproduced almost every oddity in Freud's footnotes. What is interesting in this is neither Joyce's unique personal psychology, nor indeed the secret details of the sexual relationship between the author and Nora Barnacle. On the contrary, it is the secret banality of the letters' contents that is so striking, though the prose is undoubtedly more interesting than Freud's. The overwhelming similarity indicates the historical determinacy of sexual fantasy. It also serves as a reminder of the extent to which both Joyce and Freud's texts, whether private or public, are symptomatic of their time.

In her interpretation of key aspects of the relationship between Joyce and Nora, Murphy drew on a sense of their cultural context in Trieste at the time, and of the historical conditions of desire itself: 'One of the things that's been a great source has been the experience of Trieste itself. Going there for the first time and beginning to understand how Viennese it was, thinking about what was around Joyce, what would he have been absorbing at the time. Triestine culture was permeated with *fin de siècle* Vienna, where decadence was somehow decaying into new cultural forms.' For Murphy, a striking feature of the new intellectual and artistic movements of the time was their fascination 'with human agony in relationships, in relation to sexuality'. Above all, *Nora's* realization of Trieste and Dublin examines 'the environment in which desire was acted out'. This awareness of the *fin de siècle* exploration of sexuality feeds into Murphy's play with the conventions of the costume drama genre.

Love, Letters and Fetishism

One of the most dynamic of contemporary cultural critics, Slavoj Žižek, argues that Joyce's work has a transhistorical quality of anticipation:

> The 'modernism' of Joyce resides in the fact that his works, at least *Ulysses* and *Finnegans Wake*, are not simply external to their interpretation but, as it were, in advance take into account their possible interpretations and enter into dialogue with them. Insofar as an interpretation or theoretical explanation of a work of art endeavours to 'frame' its object, one can say that this modernist dialectics provides another example of how the frame is always included in, is a part of, the framed content: in modernism, theory about the work is comprised in the work, the work is a kind of pre-emptive strike at possible theories about itself.[38]

Žižek's comments are only the most recent version of a fixed belief of much, very diverse, Joycean exegesis, that the texts are both an inexhaustible source of critical theories, but are also self-contained, infinitely full of meaning which each reading can only partially unravel. *Nora* is a film not a theory, and it is grounded in Nora's non-existent letters. In effect it refuses to fetishize the absent feminine representation of herself, instead inhabiting and representing the space, shifting the contours of reality. Which is not to say the film eschews fetishism. On the contrary, it deploys it in the articulation of desires and subjects grounded in their own history, but is not frozen in it. *Nora* shares *The Piano*'s project in important respects:

Taking traditional mechanisms of desire and modes of articulation in order to question and subvert them and, especially, to give twentieth-century feminism a voice in situations where in the past such intervention has not occurred.[39]

Murphy points out that one effect of period costume drama is that 'people are so dressed that [when they undress] by contrast they are so naked'. She explains *Nora*'s use of costume in terms of the conventions of the period and the film's central protagonists' ambivalent relation with those conventions:

It is led by the characters. If you set out to do a movie on Nora and Joyce, it follows that you are going to have to deal with costume, but you have to think about how design and costume express what you want to say in the film.

Costume is an element of the narrative's fidelity to the recorded detail of Nora and Joyce's lives, but it also indicates how they represented themselves to others and each other. This particular visual dimension to the characterization does come very much from Brenda Maddox's biography of Nora – 'She uses the photographs as a way of talking about the clothes Nora wore. Then we looked at Anthony Burgess's book of photos which tracks all the looks Joyce goes through from the ages of twenty to forty.'[40] Joyce changed his style 'the way people do now. He tried out different looks all the time. He was being the guy who hung out, then this Doestoyevskian student, then in Trieste he becomes a boulevardier, then an academic and a professorial-looking guy.' As Bruzzi points out, it is a given in modern Western society that 'the sexual effect of display has . . . been transferred to the woman'.[41] She quotes an early study of the psychology of clothes:

Man's morality tends to find expression in his clothes . . . modern man's clothing abounds in features which symbolise his devotion to the principles of duty, of renunciation and of self-control. The whole relatively 'fixed' system of his clothing is, in fact, an outward and visible sign of the strictness of his adherence to the social code.[42]

At least since the 1890s dandyism has been a strategy of refusal of duty, renunciation, self-control and fixed masculinity. Joyce's experiments with his personal appearance are part of his participation in a broader cultural movement. They also suggest a certain uneasiness with fixed identities that is also expressed in his letters. This is indicated not just in the overtly erotic letters, but also in his frequent interjections in his ordinary correspondence with Nora, when they were apart, of extraordinarily detailed descriptions of what she should wear on his return. This is a very conventional sexual game, of course: the man experiences the 'pleasures of "vicarious display"' . . . through the desired woman'.[43] But it is more complex than that, as Murphy's interpretation foregrounds. For Nora Barnacle, clothes obviously had a social and economic as well as a sexual significance: 'with her it has to do with economics as well. Starting out, they were literally incredibly poor, having all that they stood up in and no more. They associated being better off with having more and more stuff'. This sense of clothes as a complex expression of sexual desire, economic aspiration and social function informs the visual style of the film:

> Two things were guidelines for us making the movie. These were people who lived on their wits, who owned only what they stood up in, and they lived in a culture where clothing was incredibly important. When they got any money or even when they didn't have any money they ran up huge bills with clothing people. Their clothes were their homes; their clothes were where they lived, because they moved so often.

In the portrait scene, which Murphy identifies as crucial to the issue of the representation of women within the film, *Nora* looks from a feminist angle at men looking at women. The gaze of the male protagonists becomes itself the object of another's gaze, the process of subsuming the woman into the fetish object exposed to view. As Murphy points out:

> The dynamic of a portrait being painted is actually quite strange. It's not like a photograph. Someone sits there and is stared at and it can go on for days and days. I think that Nora realises how Joyce is using this convention, setting her up to be looked at by the artist, and then bringing Prezioso into this situation. It is like a stage that is set up for a certain action. And the whole thing has to do with looking at her refusing to be looked at. In terms of how the film works and in terms of the way the representation of her is made explicit, then that [portrait scene] is really the key scene.[44]

The scene and situation in the film were very much influenced by Joyce's notes for *Exiles*, where, as Murphy points out, Joyce appears to be 'doing Ibsen or Strindberg' – indeed one publisher rejected Joyce's play for being too much like Strindberg. The play closely parallels Joyce and Nora's relationship with Prezioso as presented in the film, with the returned exile and writer, Richard, basically offering his wife, Bertha, to Robert, her former admirer who has remained to become a prosperous Dubliner. Joyce's own notes on *Exiles* make the homoerotic underpinning of heterosexual triangles very explicit, while simultaneously attempting to disown homosexuality as 'dissatisfaction and degradation':

> The bodily possession of Bertha by Robert, repeated often, would certainly bring into almost carnal contact the two men. Do they desire this? To be united, that is carnally through the person and body of Bertha as they cannot, without dissatisfaction and degradation – be united carnally man to man as man to woman?[45]

This is more oblique in the play. When Robert confesses his desire for Bertha, it is obvious that it is Richard who determines the attraction: 'You love this woman. I remember all you told me long ago. She is yours, your work. (*Suddenly*.) And that is why I, too, was drawn to her. You are so strong that you attract me even through her.'[46] There is a recurrent sense of an emotional, intellectual and sexual world created by the fears and desires of one of its inhabitants. Robert repeatedly asserts that Richard has made Bertha who she is. Yet Bertha, though she ultimately desires to start again with Richard, exceeds his fiction of her. 'You do not understand anything in me', she tells him, 'not one thing in my heart or soul'. She declares, 'I am living with a stranger!' Despite his intellect and passion, so is he.

7

AN OTHER DESIRE:
SCREENING NORA FROM MOLLY

'My wife writes without regard for capitals or punctuation', exclaims Joyce in Murphy's film, which thus identifies her writing style with that of Molly Bloom. But then, by the time he came to write Molly's monologue, Nora Barnacle's husband had learnt a similar disregard for grammatical proprieties. David Lloyd has argued that *Ulysses* is an 'adulterative' fiction, a contagion at the site of the attempt to culturally produce Irish nationality as pure, total and homogenous. *Ulysses* deliberately dismantles 'the ideological verisimilitude of cultural nationalism'.[47] Joyce's use of myth is necessarily parodic, distinguishing itself from the earnest, authenticating recourse to myths of Mother Ireland and essential Irishness which characterize Irish cultural nationalism. The 'Cyclops' episode in the novel, according to Lloyd, is a passage of 'intercontamination', where the Citizen's attempt at monologic national self-representation is infected and its fragility and violent instability betrayed by 'the internal heterogeneity, the adulteration of discourses . . . the ceaseless interpenetration of different discourses'[48] which constitute *Ulysses*.

Lloyd's reading implicitly identifies Joyce and Molly Bloom: his stylistic adulterations are 'the exact aesthetic correlative of adultery in the social sphere'.[49] The promiscuous text is subsequently aligned with female sexuality:

> For if adultery is forbidden under patriarchal law, it is precisely because of the potential multiplication of possibilities for identity that it implies as against the paternal fiction, which is based on no more than legal verisimilitude.

> If the spectre of adultery must be exorcized by nationalism, it is in turn because adulteration undermines the stable formation of legitimate and authentic identities. It is not difficult to trace here the basis for nationalism's consistent policing of female sexuality by the ideological and legal confinement of women to the domestic sphere.[50]

It is not difficult to identify here a gendering of 'social' adultery as feminine and literary adulteration as masculine, which leaves women once again confined to the domestic sphere. Nevertheless, the alliance implied between the feminine, the sexual and the maternal, and the aesthetic rupture of totalizing nationalisms is one well worth exploring.

The terms of that exploration are very different in Murphy's film. For within it, Nora Barnacle's subversion of the matrix of male representation lies in her refusal of adultery. Far from being a mode of subversion, within the scenario set up by Joyce for her adultery is just another mode of confinement to be evaded, a fetish which will 'fix' and define her identity, even if she is defined as the threat to identity. There are large and fascinating differences of interpretation of the significance of adultery in the Joycean imaginary between Lloyd and Murphy, which arises from their equally different interpretations of female sexuality. Murphy is very clear that Nora cannot be defined antithetically, as the opposite of repression or convention:

> Sometimes people like Nora are represented in cinema and in literature as this earthy kind of sex goddess and that is just not all she is. It diminishes and limits her to propose that what liberates her from being a repressed, oppressed Irish woman is no more than the opposite of that image.

Adultery may be oppositional, but only to a narrowly defined fidelity. One of the things which the Prezioso episode foregrounds in

Murphy's film is that Nora's ultimate fidelity is to herself. In Murphy's version, it is precisely because Nora refuses adultery that she maintains her sexuality and identity independent of her lover:

> It is part of what I mean about her seeming to accept his image while rejecting it. It's got to do with the power of refusing to speak as well. Which is why I think the notion that feminism equals having a voice is problematic. One can have a voice by not speaking. One can have a voice by being silent, it can be as expressive as using a lot of words.

Lloyd's reading of *Ulysses* is very much rooted in the modernist construction of the feminine as a dangerous, exhilarating realm of authenticity in which the modernist artist could ground his art. While Murphy defends Joyce as always avoiding the kind of contempt for women and sexuality which often went hand in hand with this apparent celebration of feminine otherness, there is no doubt that his work operates within the context of modernism's use of the feminine as a resource at masculine aesthetic disposal.

Alice Jardine has argued that modernism makes articulation of the feminine a legitimizing strategy.[51] Forays into this dangerous territory become touchstones of daring and authenticity is claimed through recycling an old myth of immanent reality, accessing organic life through the feminine. At the same time, modernism is haunted by the fear that the other knows herself better and may have something more interesting to say. This sense of another voice, not defined by the myth or admitted to history, surfaces in 'Nausicaa'. Gertie's fantasy of the dark stranger in this episode is one which Gilbert and Gubar identify as recurrent in nineteenth-century women's literature and which they describe as 'female fantasies that are much more concerned with power and authority than romance'.[52] The language Gertie borrows from such fantasies and the other languages of popular culture which surface in the novel constitute frustrated protomyths which seek universal significance for the everyday in ways which correspond to Joyce's strategies. Though these protomyths fail, they are not treated altogether unsympathetically. The pulp romance voice of Gerty benefits by contrast with the immediately preceding spleen of the Cyclops narrator and a highly inflated passage describing Bloom in the jaunting car as ben Bloom Elijah transfigured. There is considerable poignancy in the contrast between her style and the reality of her family's impoverishment and brutalization as a result of her father's alcoholism, and the record of beatings followed by reference to piety.[53] Her romantic musings may be conventional and hypocritical, but her attraction to Bloom's foreignness is a version of that alliance of the sexual and alien which the Citizen feared. Gerty's romantic prose and devotional pieties mingle into an eroticization of and identification with the Virgin Mother, an unravelling of the myth at the textual level, but also an unwitting personal subversion of its repressive power. Gerty, like Molly, 'loved to read poetry',[54] even if her taste is sentimental and satirized.[55]

The authority of the author is always perilous and self-parodic in *Ulysses*, but the encounter with feminine self-articulation does seem to raise particular anxieties. Stephen is teased (by John Eglinton) in the National Library about dictating a new version of *Paradise Lost* to six medics – '*The Sorrows of Satan* he calls it.'[56] The title is that of a novel by Marie Corelli and the comment is followed by a false smile from Stephen. Stephen and the despised popular woman writer are associated in their illegitimate relation to a tradition defined in terms of Goethe, Shakespeare and Lyster's sense of criticism as 'A great poet on a great brother poet'.[57] Later, Eglinton will comment that 'Vining held that the prince [Hamlet] was a woman. Has no-one made him out to be an Irish-man?'[58] indicating that he is subliminally aware of the connection. In daring as well as resenting such an association, Joyce's fascination with popular, despised or corrupt cultural forms (advertising, street ballads) and his colonial sense of exclusion from a masculine realm of cultural authority fuse. Stephen's response is conventionally 'feminine', telling himself to smile at this mockery of his intellectual pretensions. Eglinton's next comment indicates that Stephen lacks something necessary to become part of the great brotherhood of poets, whether of the old imperial cultures or the emerging 'legitimate' Irish tradition, epitomized by Yeats and Synge – 'I feel you would need more for Hamlet'.[59] And after Stephen meditates on his sympathy for and alienation from Cranly's quest to free Ireland, here ambiguously gendered ('sireland', but also 'gaptoothed Kathleen'),[60] Eglinton 'censured' that, 'Our young Irish bards . . . have yet to create a figure which the world will set beside Saxon Shakespeare's *Hamlet* though I admire him, as old Ben did, on this side idolatry'.[61] Eglinton's idolatry is the desire of the colonized to culturally rival the colonizer by reproducing the colonizer's forms and it will lead others like him to censure/censor the writing of a new generation of writers that does not serve this purpose. His association of himself with Ben Jonson is ironic. Joyce implies that Ireland's literary 'renaissance' is crippled by seeing itself in terms determined by English cultural myths. Yet Jonson's 'On inviting a friend to dinner' invokes a defiant conviviality and the social paranoia induced by the presence of informers in a way which is close to Bloom's earlier musing on this subject. Writing, *Ulysses* implies, is always in danger of being on the wrong side of power.

Nevertheless, a patrilinear, authoritative Western cultural tradition has been produced in the image of political imperatives of nation, state and empire and it is from this tradition that these Irish literary sons seek recognition. It is a tradition presented with homoerotic overtones by Joyce, in the reference to Aristotle as Plato's 'schoolboy' and in the over-emphatic denial by Stephen of the possibility of a sexual betrayal of the father–son relationship: 'They are sundered by a bodily shame so steadfast that the criminal annals of the world . . . hardly record its breach.'[62] The possibility having been raised, it is difficult to ignore the ambiguity of: 'He is in my father. I am in his son.'[63] Such overtones subvert the polarity of body and mind, culture and materiality, sexuality and purity necessary to maintain the notion of an objective, universal aesthetic and cultural standard. The intellectual interchange of men is never far from erotic exchange, specifically the exchange of women as aesthetic and erotic object. This is implicit in the conversation about art and Shakespeare between Stephen and his companions outside the National Library. It is explicit in the relationship between Robert and Richard in *Exiles*. The portrait scene in *Nora* exposes this trade in images, especially images of women, drawing on the recurrent triangulations of sexual jealousy, art and anxiety throughout Joyce's work, but with a liberating and illuminating twist. Like Bertha, Nora resists. She is ultimately neither aesthetic object, sexual commodity nor social experiment, roles which are variously ascribed to her and to the female characters at the heart of other Joycean triangles. For Nora, here, is a character in a fiction formed beyond the bonds of male friendship and rivalry, in an other woman's work.

The film also draws heavily on Joyce's representation of supposedly literary, intellectual and political exchanges between men and his corrosive pictures of Dublin pub culture. *Ulysses* presents this masculine domain as one characterized by xenophobia, simmering violence and distrust, a place of exile and danger where Bloom dallies at his peril. *Nora* sketches in its Dublin scenes the snobbery, petty jealousies and sexual predatoriness of this world, so often nostalgically sentimentalized in tourist promotions of Dublin. In the film, the character of Cosgrove, who sets out to destroy Joyce and Nora's relationship by claiming she had an affair with him prior to meeting Joyce, comes to emblematize all of the reasons why Joyce had to leave Dublin. However, in dramatizing the patronizing attitudes of his fellow intellectuals in Trieste, the film is careful not to present Irish society as having any kind of exclusive patent on misogyny.

In this respect it is worth analysing in detail the episode in the café in Trieste where Nora and Joyce are entirely united in their singing of 'The Lass of Aughrim', then separated after she is patronized and insulted by one of Joyce's fellow English teachers, who tells Joyce how wrong he is to keep Nora away from everything she knows. Nora and Joyce are then reunited in the storm which rages outside. The song is not presented as part of a tradition to which Nora gives Joyce access, along the lines parodied in the activities of middle-class Irish-language activists Stephen Daedalus encounters in *Portrait of the Artist as a Young Man*. Singing the traditional (but English-language) sentimental song together is indicative of a willingness to own emotions not acceptable to the respectable societies of either Dublin or Trieste. The ballad takes the form of a dialogue, so it is art produced jointly by them, unlike his writing. The intervention of Joyce's colleague is based on the patronizing preconceptions Murphy finds so annoying. He assumes that Nora is not the agent of her own choices and is incapable of deciding to stay or leave of her own free will. Asserting herself against this, Nora flees out into the storm. When Joyce follows her, the scene echoes that of thousands of romantic films where lovers take refuge in wild nature from societal constraint. *Nora* does not play that scene, however. Joyce, for the second time in the film, is shown to be completely out of his depth in elemental nature. Nora must rush back and comfort him, so intimidated is he by nature's showy reminder of man's insignificance.

In keeping with the urban idiom of his work, Joyce is presented in the film as at odds with nature. There is no doubt his work relentlessly opposes the sentimentalization of rural life prevalent in middle-class Irish nationalism. His most famous short story, 'The Dead', goes to great lengths to present a modern urban male as a creature much more at home making dinner-party speeches than confronting the elements, from which he must be carefully protected by galoshes, overcoats, taxi cabs and the minutiae of urban life in a cold climate which Joyce's fiction so painstakingly realizes. Murphy links the Triestine storm scene with the earlier one in the film where Joyce is frightened by cattle being driven through the Dublin streets to market. The scene is fictionalized but draws on Joyce's known fears and his poem 'Tilly',[64] written in1904 when he was walking out with Nora. It is also based on Murphy's own childhood experiences living 'just down the road from north Richmond Street where "Araby" is set'. She remembers that on Wednesday mornings cattle were driven down the road to the boats. At any sudden noise, the cattle would scatter, often into tenement dwellings whose doors had been burnt for firewood: 'There was something about the way nature and the city were so closely linked that was frightening. You think you're walking in a city street and suddenly there's this kind of stampede, like an uncontrollable urge.' Murphy specifically links the storm scene in Trieste with these frightening eruptions of nature within the urban environment. As Murphy had originally written it, 'Nora comes back and pulls him into the storm'. In this version of the script, 'the café was to be on the port, with the waves breaking near it in the storm'. Shot in that way it would have had to be read in terms of a number of key scenes at the urban edge of the sea in Joyce's fiction. The cost of wave machines and the difficulty of controlling the location shooting in these circumstances forestalled a whole set of Joycean references in a manner which draws attention to the way in which practical and financial considerations condition cinematic images. Shot as it is, 'it's about his fear of the elements and his connecting her with this elemental kind of thing'. The couple's reunion in the storm-ridden street both registers this perception on his part and rebukes it in the representation of Nora's amused affection for him and his eccentricities, which defuses all the previous angry intensity. Their relationship is not outside of society nor does it have the tragic destiny usually associated in literature and film with lovers who are at one with storms and the sea. While the couple are socially marginalized, the film also celebrates the way in which they find their way in and around society.

Penelope and the Art of Unravelling

In Ulysses, Mulligan mocks Yeats's ecstatic description of Lady Gregory's Poets and Dreamers – 'One thinks of Homer'[65] – but the comment also anticipates similar mockery of Joyce's own pretensions in writing his Homeric novel. Joyce's writing often opposes feminine existence to masculine art and often generates its own avant-garde authority in a parodic relation to popular forms associated with women. Underlying this, however, is an engagement with feminine forms of subjectivity and expression. The alliance or identification that I am arguing for here between Joyce and the woman writer is attested to in Angela Carter's humorous use of Joycean references in Wise Children,[66] for example, and in the readings of Joyce by Kristeva and Cixous which see him as a writer who 'gets something by' of woman and as an ally in the feminine attempt to re-negotiate the socio-symbolic order. Nora then is a rare, brave and critical attempt to exploit this resource from a specifically Irish perspective. Like Angela Carter, Murphy adopts a dual approach, using Joycean elements in a very different way and both positively exploring and clear-mindedly deconstructing his representations of women.

The confrontation between Bloom and the Citizen in *Ulysses* is a scene of unravelling identities. The latter's comment that a faithless wife was 'the cause of all our misfortune'[67] applies so aptly to Leopold Bloom's personal predicament that this Irish myth of betrayal becomes in the same gesture personalized, depoliticized and repoliticized. It undermines Bloom's exclusion from the group, since their myths have relevance for him. It unmasks the insecurity of pure forms of identity and the wellsprings of the need for scapegoats. The assembled company in this scene might laugh at the idea that they are strangers to themselves, but the suspicion that their wives are strangers to them surfaces uneasily. Male obsession with female fidelity runs through all the scenes set in the claustrophobia of literary pub culture in Murphy's film. *Nora* celebrates Joyce's reversal of this need to know absolutely which runs through his own jealous obsessions, but is ultimately inverted.

Identification of *Ulysses'* textual strategies with Molly Bloom's infidelities begs identification between Joyce and Penelope. Like

Molly, Penelope is an artist and like Joyce she is an artist primarily concerned with undoing. Weaving and unweaving, making decision and desire wait upon an achievement she constantly undoes, Penelope is more than a figure for the novel's 'adulterations' of tradition. She provides a myth of writing which will supersede Dedalus to become central to *Finnegans Wake*.

The representation and subversion of the eternal feminine and her relation to Mother Ireland is a key site of cultural unravelling, enacted early in *Ulysses* and recurring until it is defined and completed in Molly's monologue. The encounter between Stephen, Haines and Mulligan and the milk-woman at the very beginning of the novel prefigures all of the contradictions and paradoxes that will be resolved, however unsatisfactorily, by Molly. The milk-woman, defined by giving nurture and 'her woman's unclean loins',[68] is a stereotypical figure of the maternal, needed and feared. She takes the narrative place of Athene, but never achieves mythic status, for she is mocked even before her entrance by Mulligan's recounting of an old Dublin saying: 'When I makes tea I makes tea, as old Mother Grogan said. And when I makes water I makes water. . . so I do Mrs Cahill, says she. Begob ma'am, says Mrs Cahill, god send you don't make them in the same pot.'[69] This is Molly's meditation on her breasts' fascination for the men in her life and her excretions and effusions prefigured and condensed. The old woman's voice is mimicked by Mulligan; Joyce will construct Molly's.

Sayings are the most fragmentary aspect of the oral tradition, the very opposite to the complex but highly coherent set of images implied by myth, particularly the myth of the eternal feminine. No simple opposition is posited in *Ulysses* between the local and folkloric and the conservative and universal myth, however. The old woman is also very specifically Mother Ireland: 'Silk of the kine and poor old woman names given her in old times'.[70] And Stephen prefigures the Citizen's paranoid logic in describing her (he reprises this in 'Oxen of the Sun'): 'A wandering crone. Serving her conqueror and gay betrayer.'[71] The mythic burden of this figure is comically overloaded when the milk-woman mistakes the Irish addressed to her by the Englishman Haines for French. Her mistake oddly aligns her with Stephen, even as he scorns her, for he, not willing to wait for her milk, wanted lemon in his tea: 'damn you and your Paris fads', comments Mulligan.[72] This perplexity of national identities does not simply debunk the myth of Mother Ireland. That is left to Mulligan, who is heartily despised for his crudity here. The residual power of the myth is evident in Stephen's recoil from this woman's subservience and understanding of the encounter in mythic terms, an understanding which neatly removes from the men the responsibility for an understanding of economic terms and full payment of the bill. At the heart of the exchange between the old stereotype and the modern parodists is an ironic sense that 'Ireland is just another of those modern places, where there is no *there* any more'.[73]

In *Finnegan's Wake*, Joyce moves beyond Molly. Anna Livia Plurabelle is another universal and particular myth of the feminine, but she is also 'full of sillymottocraft'[74] and she imagines alternatives: 'how the wilde amazia . . . she would seize to my other breast.'[75] Her closing lament, 'And its old and old its sad and old its sad and weary I go back to you, my cold father [sea] . . . and I rush my only into your arms' echoes the lament of the Cailleach Bheara, a mythic and prototypical Mother Ireland poem, but this Anna Livia is nobody's sovereignty goddess: 'How can you own water really? It's always flowing in a stream, never the same.'[76]

Anna Livia's acronym offers another figure for writing, of folkloric rather than mythic origin. The *alp luachra* in Irish folklore gets into the stomachs of men who lie down in cut grass and breeds there. She and her children can only be expelled through regurgitation over a stream. The story turns up in Douglas Hyde's *Beside the Fire: a Collection of Irish Gaelic Stories*, published in 1910.[77] Hyde was famous for sanitizing these stories, but the impregnating maternal *alp luachra* is a scandalous figure, as confusing as tea and water in the same pot, crossing genders and eliciting an abject regurgitation which parallels Joyce's own compulsive quotation, appropriation and reproduction. And she has precedents, particularly in the erotic letters which Joyce sent Nora in 1909 and 1912. Murphy comments of these that:

> In the movie it's a time when they are physically separate, yet you are aware of an incredible closeness between them. I feel they used the letters to hold on to each other when they were physically apart. So the most sexualized parts of the movie in terms of their relationship is actually not when they're together, it's when they are apart from each other. That really interested me.

Nora puts this exchange of letters at the heart of its reinterpretation of the relationship between them. Murphy has commented that her initial reaction to the letters was 'how can he lay all this shit on this woman?'[78] Brenda Maddox's was similar. The disgust quotient cannot be underestimated in assessing critical responses to the letters. The Joyce family's objection to their publication is well known and outlined in great detail in Maddox's book. Such commentary as there has been has tended to concentrate on their evidence of a variety of psychosexual obsessions on Joyce's part. Murphy's film reflects, however, a much more complex response. As she points out, Nora wrote back. While this is more than proven by Joyce's frequent references to her replies to him, Nora's letters themselves do not appear to be extant. As Murphy notes:

> You can never get to her separate from him. You always have to use him as a way into her and that's one of the reasons *Nora* is not a feminist film in the sense that *Anne Devlin* and *Maeve* are feminist films. . . . It is not trying to recuperate her and say that she was something else.

For Maddox, interestingly, Nora's participation in these fantasies is both manipulative and degrading. She argues that Nora, insecure in her position as the absence of marriage would inevitably make a woman of her era, ensured Joyce's fidelity and his return to her from Ireland by catering to his more bizarre sexual requests. The film refers extensively to the frightening position of dependence on Joyce in which Nora found herself once she arrived in Trieste, but it does not ultimately wish to see Nora's decision to stay with Joyce as one necessitated by this dependence. Maddox's reaction to the letters implies a very different view of the relationship between sex and money, or rather between sexual and commodity fetishism, than the one Murphy proposes twelve years later. The latter comments that she read the letters a lot: 'It was quite a shock. When I started working on *Nora* I had not read the letters, but once you know they are there, you can't leave them out.' Commenting that it is a particular interpretation of 'what's going on in those letters that is the source' used in the film 'rather than the letters themselves', Murphy remarks that 'The letters helped provide this structure, focusing the story on things like jealousy and hope and the ways people hold on to each other erotically . . . at the times where they are being most open and naked with each other'.

This exchange of letters and their relation to desire is, on one level, exemplary fetishism. The letters take the place of the remote object of desire. But this is a fetishistic exchange, they write back and forth, responding to each other. Who is the object and who is the subject? Maddox's sense of Nora's exploitation, her indignation that this is not fair exchange, is grounded in her sense of Nora's economic dependence and on the inevitable effect of the absence of Nora's actual letters. The film moves to balance this effect by faking the absent letters. It restores the balance of erotic trade, so to speak. This is oddly facilitated by the exigencies of copyright restrictions on Joyce's original letters. Refused permission to quote directly, Murphy and her collaborator on the script, Gerry Stembridge, faked all the letters, both Joyce and Nora's. This is glorious postmodern presumption and it liberates the film from the ultimate fetish of literary adaptation, that of obsessional fidelity to the original word.

Interestingly it also makes the feminist filmmaker the author of textual adulteration, which Lloyd couched in masculine terms in opposition to Molly Bloom's embedded femininity. Murphy remarks:

> The thing about the absence of her letters, as Brenda Maddox says, is that you can work out what the content of her letters were from his response. The letters are almost like a call and response, a game really. Not being able to use them, what we had to do was look at how they were functioning in the narrative and write letters that could respond to that. They are not as good obviously, but the odd thing is that people actually think they are Joyce's letters and they are neither as pornographic nor as good.

This rhythm of call and response is dramatized in the film in the scene where 'The Lass of Aughrim', a ballad about seduction and betrayal, which was obviously important to both Joyce and Nora, is sung by the two together in Trieste (see Plate 15). It also figures strongly in the scene in the film where a row between Nora and Joyce is ended by her recitation of one of his poems (Plates 16 and 17).

Plate 15. Joyce playing The Lass of Aughrim

The scene begins with Nora – pregnant, scared and extremely angry – arguing with Joyce, who lies drunkenly in bed. He says, 'I write for you' and, as Murphy describes it, 'she's just wiping the floor

Plate 16. Nora reciting poem

Plate 17. Joyce in bed, listening the her recitation

with him'. Then he quotes to her the well-known episode 'when he's tearing up a story and she just says is all that paper going to be wasted'. Murphy remarks that 'rows between couples are strictly choreographed. You are not saying you want the relationship to end, just to let them know you are really pissed off with them and you want their behaviour to change.' This row between Nora and Joyce starts in that way, but then exceeds it:

> She realizes from what he has said that they have gone very far. When that happens you have to work out how to get back. And what she does is quote the poem from *Chamber Music* and from what I've read he weeps because he realizes that she does know who he is. There is a real ambiguity there, because there are moments when he does want to get away from her, just because it could be so suffocating. There's a sort of feeling of 'now I'll never get away; she does know who I am'.

There is a further twist in the film's realization of this scene: 'We of course couldn't use that [poem from *Chamber Music*], so Gerry Stembridge wrote the poem we used and [. . .] lots of people think it's a poem by Joyce and it's a shame we couldn't use the real one.'

The episode as Murphy describes it confounds an opposition of subject and object, reader and text. For one thing, the author's words are given meaning for him when they are spoken by a (significant) other. Nora uses his words, but in doing so she defines him, not the other way round. She does it in the context of insisting on the materiality of art: literature is just so much paper after all, until it is read. 'And then', as Murphy remarks, 'there's what it means to him to hear her voice saying it'. If the row and its resolution are strictly choreographed, the choreography lies in the interplay of the two protagonists, with a blurring of the boundaries between subject and object, speaker and listener. The resolution through her quotation of him is then an act of appropriation of his words by Nora and, through

Nora, by the filmmaker. For this, after all, is not the originary text but a reading of the text's origins. The scene is, on one level, a culmination of the love story, on another an eroticization of the act of interpretation. Nora is the unforestall-able critic. It challenges the concept of the Joycean text as a hall of mirrors where all interpretation is foreseen and deflected and consequently the view of the work of art as contained, achieved and complete. Joyce in this interpretation also needs his audience, however singular, for his work to have meaning, especially to himself. It is through surrendering it to the reader/lover that this is achieved. Within the relationship of Joyce and Nora, then, the film engages with the relationship between art and interpretation. It is also profoundly at odds with modernist aesthetics, proposing against the idea of the 'organic' work of art (produced by a single consciousness) that of a dialogical art, a fetishist production to be sure, but one of love not dominance, open to and formed by the artist's environs and history, shaped by the desire for the perfect reader.

Saying 'Yes'

One of the criticisms levelled at *The Piano* was that it eroticized relations founded on economic inequality: Ada has nothing to trade for the return of her piano but sexual favours. This is very close to Maddox's interpretation of Nora's role in the exchange of erotic letters with James Joyce. Both of these criticisms touch on the relationship between sexual and commodity fetishism. After all, the most fetishized objects are also consumer goods: velvet, furs, shoes. Indeed, there is a persistent link between luxury and desire in the letters, accentuated by the juxtaposition of the abject, physical and excremental with their opposites. Perhaps cinematic tolerance of this link between economics and desire is based on its own nature. As Mulvey observes:

> The cinema, too, has insides less sightly and fascinating than its screen. It is a machine that can only work with money,

and that produces a commodity for circulation in the market, one which must also disguise the labour that created it, and its own creaky, unwieldy mechanics while it waits to be ultimately overwhelmed by electronics.[79]

This analogy between the cinema and the representation of femininity in cinema illuminates *Nora*'s self-reflexive quality. Substituting cinema as an emotional agent for poetry and song in the scene where Nora first tells Joyce of Michael Furey, Murphy is justly proud that she used films shown by Joyce in his ill-fated venture into cinema management at The Volta. The cinematic moment displaces its sources, authenticating the gesture by an attention to historical detail which foregrounds cinema's own role in the original story.

Asked about *Nora*'s representation of women, and especially Irish women, and its dialogue with the way women have been represented in Irish film, Murphy describes the relationship between Nora and her many representations as a kind 'of dance between the images that are projected on her and what she accepts and what she rejects, what she takes and then mirrors back'. In identifying sexual and artistic freedom, the film adheres to a consistent theme in Irish literature. In deploying and subverting the conventions of the historical romance, it challenges current Irish filmmaking practice. *Nora* is ultimately not an adaptation of a single literary source, but a complex web of intertextual reference and analysis. As such, it is an appropriately postmodern elegy for the modernist project it celebrates and questions. Nora ends with a woman with limited options saying 'yes'. In Murphy's film, there is, independent of the biographical impulse linked to its treatment of Joyce and Nora, a postulation of a feminine desire that is possible, limited by the material circumstances of existence no doubt, but neither beyond presentation nor representation.

CREDITS

Title:	Nora
Director	Pat Murphy
Release Year:	2000
Production Company	GAM
	Natural Nylon Entertainment
	Road Movies Filmproduktion
	Volta Films
Country	Ireland, U.K., Italy, Germany

Cast:

Susan Lynch	Nora Barnacle
Ewan McGregor	James Joyce
Andrew Scott	Michael Bodkin
Vincent McCabe	Uncle Tommy
Veronica Duffy	Annie Barnacle
Aedin Moloney	Eva Joyce
Pauline McLynn	Miss Kennedy
Neilí Conroy	Maid
Darragh Kelly	Cosgrave
Alan Devine	Gogarty
Peter McDonald	Stanislaus Joyce
Paul Hickey	Curran
Kate O'Toole	Miss Delahunty
Martin Murphy	George Russell
Karl Scully	John McCormack

Credits

Pat Murphy	Director
Bradley Adams	Producer
Damon Bryant	Producer
Guy Collins	Executive producer
Brenda Maddox	Book by
Pat Murphy	Screenplay
Gerard Stembridge	
Ulrich Felsberg	Co-producer
James Flynn	Co-producer
Tiernan MacBride	Producer Volta Films

Ewan McGregor	Co-producer
Gherardo Pagliei	Co-producer
Tracey Seaward	Producer
Stanislas Syrewicz	Original Music
Jean-François Robin	Cinematography
Pia Di Ciaula	Film Editor
Alan MacDonald	Production Designer
Stefano Maria Ortolani	Art Director
Alessandra Querzola	Set Decoration
Consolata Boyle	Costume Design
Orla Carrol	Key hair stylist
Joan Giacomin	Assistant makeup artist
Roisin O'Reilly	Assistant makeup artist
Maire O'Sullivan	Key makeup artist
Andrea Borella	Production supervisor
Marco Giacalone	Unit manager
Des Martin	Production manager
Gilles Cannatella	Second assistant director
Jill Dempsey	Assistant director
Tommy Gormley	Assistant director
Lars Henning	Assistant director
Eoin Holohan	Trainee assistant director
Lisa Kelly	Assistant director
Sarah Purser	Assistant director
Fiona Mary Spillard	Third assistant director: Italy
Boyana Sutic	Assistant director
Daniel Bacciu	Props: Italy
Stephen Daly	Assistant art director
Tamara Marini	Assistant art director
Terry Pritchard	Supervising art director
Nick Adams	Supervising sound editor
Ulrike Münch	Assistant sound editor
Adrian Rhodes	Sound re-recording mixer
Hani Al Yousif	Digital effects artist: Mill Film London
Nicholas Atkinson	Visual effects editor: Mill Film London
Karl Mooney	Digital effects supervisor: Mill Film London
Dominic Sidoli	Visual effects coordinator: Mill Film London
Beatrice Arweiler	Location manager
Ciarán Barry	Director of photography: second unit

Elisabetta Bartolomei	Production coordinator: Italy
Alan Butler	Focus puller: second unit
Carmela Compagnone	Payroll accountant
John Conroy	Assistant camera
John Conroy	Focus puller
Rose-Marie Couture	Production assistant
John Higgins	Supervising gaffer
Julia Jones	Unit publicist
James Lingard	First assistant editor

Running Time	106 mins
Colour Code	Colour

Notes

1. Brenda Maddox, *Nora* (London: Hamish Hamilton, 1988).
2. 'I don't think you can take the book and then compare it to the movie – say this is the book and this is where the film is not like the book – because it is not too interesting to me, it's not a central thing to pursue, it's very limited' (Pat Murphy, interview with author, 22 March 2003). Hereafter, quotes from Murphy are from this interview unless otherwise specified.
3. Plenary Address, 'Celebrating Irish Women's Writing', WERRC Conference, University College Dublin, May 1999.
4. Letter to Stanislaus Joyce, 3 December 1904, in *Selected Letters of James Joyce*, ed. Richard Ellman (London: Faber, 1975). See, for example, the discussion of this in Kevin Barry's *The Dead* in this series (Cork: Cork University Press, 2001).
5. *The Married Man: a Biography of D. H. Lawrence* (London: Sinclair-Stevenson, 1994) and *George's Ghosts: a Life of W. B. Yeats* (London: Picador, 1999). In a repeat of the marketing strategy for *Nora*, the Yeat's book was published in the US under the title *Yeats' Ghosts* (New York: HarperCollins, 1999).
6. Brenda Maddox, *Rosalind Franklin: the Dark Lady of DNA* (London: HarperCollins, 2002).
7. As both the biography and film concur, Nora is likely to have herself suggested she come with him, but his letters after their departure indicate he doubted if she really would follow through on this.
8. Maddox, p. 66.
9. Maria Luddy and Dympna McLoughlin, 'Women and Emigration from Ireland from the Seventeenth Century', *The Field Day Anthology of Irish Writing: Women's Writing And Traditions*, vol. 5 (Cork: Cork University Press, 2002), p. 567
10. Luddy and McLoughlin, pp. 568–569.
11. Ruth Barton, *Irish Cinema*, National Cinemas Series (London and New York: Routledge, 2004).
12. Publicity posters for *The Magdalene Sisters.*
13. Marjorie Garber, *Vice Versa* (New York: Simon and Schuster, 1995; London: Hamish Hamilton, 1996).
14. In the notes to *Exiles*, dated 13 November 1913, Joyce summarizes this: 'Moon: Shelley's grave in Rome. He is rising from it: blond she weeps for him. He has fought in vain for an ideal and died killed by the world. Yet he rises. Graveyard at Rahoon by moonlight where

Bodkin's grave is. He lies in the grave. She sees his tomb (family vault) and weeps. The name is homely. Shelley's is strange and wild. He is dark, unrisen, killed by love and life, young. The earth holds him. Bodkin died. Kearns died. In the convent they called her the man-killer (woman-killer was one of her names for me). I live in soul and body.' See Robert M. Adams, 'Light on Joyce's *Exiles*? a New MS, a Curious Analogue, and Some Speculations', *Studies In Bibliography*, 1964.

15. Pat Murphy, quoted in Margaret Ward, 'In Conversation with Pat Murphy, Anne Crilly and Margo Harkin', *Filming Women: Irish Women and Film*, publication of the Belfast Film Festival 2003, p. 21.

16. Homi K. Bhabha, 'DissemiNation: Time, Narrative, and the Margins of the Modern Nation', in *Nation and Narration*, ed. Homi K. Bhabha, (London: Routledge, 1990), p. 293.

17. Seminar at the Centre for Film Studies, University College Dublin, March 2002.

18. Murphy remarks that now it's 'changing utterly, but there seems to have been a lot of writing by Joyceans about Joyce in which Trieste is just left out as a presence. And since he is the great writer of cities that seems to be a big, big mistake.' John McCourt's *The Years of Bloom: James Joyce in Trieste 1904–1920* (Dublin: Lilliput, 2000) has been a significant intervention redressing this balance.

19. Laura Mulvey, *Fetishism and Curiosity* (London: British Film Institute; Bloomington, IN; Indiana University Press, 1996), p. 11.

20. They are of course not unique in the attempt. See for example Julie Dash's *Daughters of the Dust* (1991).

21. Lance Pettitt, *December Bride* (Cork: Cork University Press, 2001), p. 22.

22. Pettitt, *December Bride*, p. 72.

23. 'You know Mr Houlihan, the man who offered her the condom when she was working in the hotel, we actually had that, but we left it out because we didn't have time, and it's something that I think is missing because it reinforces that idea of the web of predatory men and it reinforces her love for Joyce because he's not seeing her in that way. Her experience of men is of it being dark. These are people who want things from her and sexuality becomes a kind of a transaction.' Pat Murphy, Interview, 22 March 2003.

24. Most significant debate on costume drama occurs in the context of general studies of costume, such as the ground-breaking *Fabrications: Costume and the Female Body*, eds. Jane Gaines and C. Herzog (London: Routledge, 1990); Stella Bruzzi's *Undressing Cinema:*

Clothing and Identity in the Movies (London and New York: Routledge, 1997); and Sarah Street's *Costume and Cinema* (London: Wallflower, 2001).

25. Bruzzi, *Undressing Cinema*, p. 49.
26. Bruzzi, *Undressing Cinema*, p. 49.
27. Bruzzi, *Undressing Cinema*, p. 49.
28. Bruzzi, *Undressing Cinema*, p. 51.
29. Bruzzi, *Undressing Cinema*, p. 57.
30. Bruzzi, *Undressing Cinema*, p.57.
31. Mulvey, *Fetishism and Curiosity*, p. 14.
32. Bruzzi, *Undressing Cinema*, p. 37
33. See Emer Nolan, *James Joyce and Nationalism* (London: Routledge, 1996), pp. 163–181, for a critique of this tendency in feminist readings of Joyce.
34. Declan Kiberd, *Inventing Ireland: the Literature of the Modern Nation* (London: Vintage, 1996), p. 355.
35. Julia Kristeva, *The Revolution in Poetic Language*, trans. M. Waller (New York: Columbia University Press, 1984); first published as *La Révolution du Langage Poétique* (Paris: Editions du Seuil, 1974).
36. Joyce, *Dubliners* (1914, London: Granada Panther), p. 189.
37. Žižek, *The Plague of Fantasies* (London/New York: Verso, 1997), p. 94.
38. *Lacanian Ink*, Slavoj Žižek, From Joyce-the-Symptom to the Symptom of Power.htm (1996–97).
39. Bruzzi, *Undressing Cinema*, p. 57.
40. Anthony Burgess
41. Bruzzi, *Undressing Cinema*, p. 57.
42. J. C. Flugel, *The Psychology of Clothes* (London: Hogarth, 1930), p. 113.
43. Bruzzi, *Undressing Cinema*, p. 57. The reference to vicarious display comes from Flugel.
44. 'I think it's fictionalized in the sense that the portrait is painted and the ambiguity of the relationship with Prezioso's and Joyce's work, his interest in jealousy and that kind of disruption between couples, is all happening around 1912. Also around that period they did send their children away – he wanted to send their children away to the country – it seemed to me that they sent their children away because they had a woman working for them who lived in the country. She took the children there and then they didn't want to come back. Then Nora is asking constantly for Joyce to bring the children back. She says "I want my children back, I want my son with me." And Giorgio really hurts her because he doesn't want to come back, he's

a small boy having a good time. From my point of view it just seemed like a curious number of elements to work with in terms of putting the narrative of this particular period together. Joyce is introducing this character and is clearing the stage by sending the children away.'
Pat Murphy, Interview, 22 March 2003.

45.   See Adams, 1964.
46.   See Adams, 1964.
47.   Lloyd, *Anomalous States: Irish Writing and the Post-Colonial Moment*, (Dublin: Lilliput, 1993) p. 109.
48.   Lloyd, *Anomalous States*, p. 107.
49.   Lloyd, *Anomalous States*, p. 109.
50.   Lloyd, *Anomalous States*, p. 109.
51.   Alice Jardine, *Gynesis: Configurations of Woman and Modernity* (Ithaca, NY, and London: Cornell University Press, 1985). Emer Nolan has convincingly applied this critique of modernism's deployment of the feminine to Joyce's work in *James Joyce and Nationalism* (London: Routledge, 1996), p. 164.
52.   Sandra Gilbert and Susan Gubar, *The Madwoman in the Attic: the Woman Writer and the Nineteenth Century Literary Imagination* (New Haven, CT: Yale University Press, 1979), p. 136.
53.   Joyce, *Ulysses*, (1922; Harmondsworth: Penguin, 1996), pp. 460–461.
54.   Joyce, *Ulysses*, p. 473.
55.   See Gerardine Meaney, *(Un)Like Subjects: Women, Theory, Fiction* (London: Routledge, 1993), for a discussion of the relation between Bloom's masturbatory fantasy and Joyce's authorial distance from Gerty.
56.   Joyce, *Ulysses*, p. 235.
57.   Joyce, *Ulysses*, p. 235.
58.   Joyce, *Ulysses*, p. 254.
59.   Joyce, *Ulysses*, p. 235.
60.   Joyce, *Ulysses*, p. 236.
61.   Joyce, *Ulysses*, p. 236.
62.   Joyce, *Ulysses*, p. 266.
63.   Joyce, *Ulysses*, p. 248.
64.   Joyce, In *Pomes Penyeach (*London: Faber & Faber, 1933).
65.   Joyce, *Ulysses*, p. 278.
66.   Angela Carter, *Wise Children* (London: Chatto & Windus, 1991; New York: Farrar, Strauss, Giroux, 1992).
67.   Joyce, *Ulysses*, p. 240.
68.   Joyce, *Ulysses*, p. 16.
69.   Joyce, *Ulysses*, pp. 13–14. The folklorist, Patricia Lysaght, has noted

that this saying is recorded in the Archive of the Department of Irish Folklore at University College Dublin, which indicates it was a folk saying in popular usage.

70. Joyce, *Ulysses*, p. 15.
71. Joyce, *Ulysses*, p. 15.
72. Joyce, *Ulysses*, p. 13.
73. Kiberd, *Inventing Ireland*, p. 337.
74. Joyce, *Finnegans Wake*, p. 623.
75. Joyce, *Finnegans Wake*, p. 627.
76. Joyce, *Ulysses*, p. 193.
77. Hyde is much satirized in 'Cyclops', but there is also warm reference to the Gaelic poet, Raftery, whose work became available to Joyce and his contemporaries through Hyde's translations.
78. Murphy, conversation with the author, March 2002
79. Mulvey, *Fetishism and Curiosity*, p. 94.

Bibliography

Adams, Robert M. 'Light on Joyce's *Exiles*? a New MS, a Curious Analogue, and Some Speculations', in *Studies in Bibliography*. 1964.

Barry, Kevin. *The Dead* (Cork: Cork University Press, 2001).

Barton, Ruth. *Irish Cinema* (London: Routledge, 2004).

Bhabha, Homi K. 'DissemiNation: Time, Narrative, and the Margins of the Modern Nation' in *Nation and Narration*, ed. Homi K. Bhabha (London: Routledge, 1990).

Bruzzi, Stella. *Undressing Cinema: Clothing and Identity in the Movies* (London and New York: Routledge, 1997).

Carter, Angela. *Wise Children* (London: Chatto & Windus, 1991; New York: Farrar, Strauss, Giroux, 1992).

Corelli, Marie. *The Sorrows of Satan, or, the Strange Experience of One Geoffrey Tempest, Millionaire: a Romance* (London: Methuen, 1895, ninth edition).

Flugel, J. C. *The Psychology of Clothes* (London: Hogarth, 1930).

Gaines, Jane and C. Herzog (eds.), *Fabrications: Costume and the Female Body* (London: Routledge, 1990).

Garber, Marjorie. *Vice Versa* (New York: Simon and Schuster, 1995; London: Hamish Hamilton, 1996).

Gilbert, Sandra, and Susan Gubar, *The Madwoman in the Attic: the Woman Writer and the Nineteenth Century Literary Imagination* (New Haven, CT: Yale University Press, 1979).

Jardine, Alice. *Gynesis: Configurations of Woman and Modernity*. (Ithaca, NY, and London: Cornell University Press, 1985).

Joyce, James. *A Portrait of the Artist as a Young Man* (London: Egoist Press, 1916).

——. *Chamber Music* (London: Elkin Matthews, 1907).

——. *Dubliners* (1914; London: Granada Panther, 1967).

——. *Exiles* (London: Grant Richards, 1918).

——. *Finnegan's Wake* (1939; Harmondsworth: Penguin, 1992).

——. *Letters of James Joyce*, ed. Stuart Gilbert (London: Faber, 1957–66).

——. *Pomes Penyeach* (London: Faber & Faber, 1933).

——. *Selected Letters of James Joyce*, ed. Richard Ellman (London: Faber, 1975).

——. *Ulysses.* (1922; Harmondsworth: Penguin, 1996).

Kiberd, Declan. *Inventing Ireland: the Literature of the Modern Nation* (London: Vintage, 1996).

Kristeva, Julia. *The Revolution in Poetic Language*, trans. M. Waller (New York: Columbia University Press, 1984); first published as *La Révolution du Langage Poétique* (Paris: Editions du Seuil, 1974).

——. *Strangers to Ourselves*, trans. Leon S Roudiez (Hemel Hempstead: Harvester Wheatsheaf, 1991).

Lloyd, David. *Anomalous States: Irish Writing and the Post-Colonial Moment* (Dublin: Lilliput, 1993).

Luddy, Maria, and Dympna McLoughlin, 'Women and Emigration from Ireland from the Seventeenth Century', in *The Field Day Anthology of Irish Writing: Women's Writing and Traditions*, Vol. 5 (Cork: Cork University Press, 2002), pp. 567–588.

Maddox, Brenda. *Nora* (London: Hamish Hamilton, 1988; Boston: Houghton Mifflin, 1988).

——. *The Married Man: a Biography of D. H. Lawrence* (London: Sinclair-Stevenson, 1994).

——. *George's Ghosts: a Life of W. B. Yeats* (London: Picador, 1999); *Yeats' Ghosts* (New York: HarperCollins, 1999).

——. *Rosalind Franklin: the Dark Lady of DNA* (London: HarperCollins, 2002).

Meaney, Gerardine. *(Un)Like Subjects: Women, Theory, Fiction* (London: Routledge, 1993).

Mulvey, Laura. 'Visual Pleasure and Narrative Cinema', *Screen* Vol. 16, No. 3 (1975), pp. 6–18.

——. *Fetishism and Curiosity* (London: British Film Institute; Bloomington, IN: Indiana University Press, 1996).

Nolan, Emer. *James Joyce and Nationalism* (London: Routledge, 1996).

Pettitt, Lance. *December Bride* (Cork: Cork University Press, 2001).

Street, Sarah. *Costume and Cinema* (London: Wallflower, 2001).

Ward, Margaret. 'In Conversation with Pat Murphy, Anne Crilly and Margo Harkin', in *Filming Women: Irish Women and Film*, publication of the Belfast Film Festival 2003, p. 21.

Žižek, Slavoj. *The Plague of Fantasies* (London, New York: Verso, 1997)

——. *Lacanian Ink*, 'From Joyce-the-Symptom to the Symptom of Power'.htm (1996–97).